Dog and Gun

Dog and Gun

A Few Loose Chapters on Shooting,

Among Which Will Be Found
Some Anecdotes and Incidents

Johnson J. Hooper

With an Introduction by
Philip D. Beidler

The University of Alabama Press
Tuscaloosa and London

Library of Congress Cataloging-in-Publication Data

Hooper, Johnson Jones, 1815–1862.
    Dog and gun : a few loose chapters on shooting, among which will
be found some anecdotes and incidents / Johnson J. Hooper ; with an
introduction by Philip D. Beidler.
        p.   cm. — (The Library of Alabama classics)
    Reprint. Originally published: New York : Orange Judd, 1856.
    ISBN 0-8173-0561-0 (alk. paper)
    1. Fowling.   2. Shooting.   3. Bird dogs—Training.   I. Title.
II. Series.
SK313.H78   1992
799.2'4'097509034—dc20   91-21116

British Library Cataloguing-in-Publication Data available

CONTENTS.

CHAPTER VI.

CHAPTER VII.

CHAPTER VIII.

CHAPTER IX.

CHAPTER X.

CHAPTER XI.

CHAPTER XII.

CHAPTER XIII.

INTRODUCTION.

PHILIP D. BEIDLER

By 1856, when Johnson J. Hooper, author of the legendary *Adventures of Captain Simon Suggs*, sought to publish a comparatively "serious" volume, *Dog and Gun*, one of his motives seems to have been certain: he had grown tired of being known as Johnson J. Hooper, author of the legendary *Adventures of Captain Simon Suggs*. It was one matter, he had discovered, to bask in the genial celebrity of being automatically associated with his back-country rapscallion and confidence-man *extraordinaire*. It was another, as his biographers have reported, when people confused him with his creation. His runaway success as a premier Southwestern Humorist had backfired into a crisis of literary *and* personal identity.

This situation must have been particularly galling to the erudite Whig lawyer, journalist, judge, and politician who had created his crass, illiterate, unprincipled hero as the ultimate low-life Democrat; and who had created him, moreover, in a book intended to be a satire of the kind of campaign biography popular with the Jacksonian mobocracy.

Coming from a respectable newspaper family in Wilmington, North Carolina, educating himself in law, and marrying in 1842 the daughter of a rich East Alabama merchant-planter, Hooper had quickly moved from legal practice to editorship of the *East Alabamian*, Chambers County's only newspaper, and then to broader renown for humorous stories published in New York sporting journals such as

William T. Porter's *Spirit of the Times*. Shortly there followed the extraordinary success of *Simon Suggs*, editorships of the Wetumpka *Whig* and Montgomery *Alabama Journal* and *Mail*, further law practice and a solicitorship of the Ninth Circuit, and final wartime service in Richmond until his death in 1862 as Secretary of the Confederate Congress. Along the way had also come another popular book of humorous stories, *A Ride With Old Kit Kuncker*, published in Tuscaloosa in 1849, and reissued in 1851 with some new additions by a Philadelphia publisher as *The Widow Rugby's Husband*.

Amidst this crowded record of achievement, vocational and literary, *Dog and Gun* remains, of all the author's works, the least known to the scholar or the general reader. Such obscurity persists even though it enjoyed a commercial publication life exceeded only by that of *Simon Suggs*, going through one complete newspaper series, appearing in six book editions between 1856 and 1871, and staying in print until 1876. The reasons for the neglect are several and complex. First, the book has been simply hard to find. Second, despite multiple invocations of William T. Porter and thus the prestige of other well-known "sporting" titles such as the latter's popular anthology, *The Big Bear of Arkansas*, or A. B. Longstreet's *Georgia Scenes*, it makes few pretensions to other than a straightfaced, utilitarian purpose. It seems altogether a serious volume on a practical, manly subject. (The title page, for instance, bears the imprimatur of Orange, Judd, and Company, "Agricultural Publishers." Examples of other texts in the "line" may be gleaned from advertisements in the back for such offerings as "Gardening for Profit" and "The Grape Culturist.") Third, this dissipation of "literary" authority is also abetted internally by the work's status as a rather miscellaneous book, almost an anthology. It is of course written mainly by Hooper himself; and when he is there, he is in good voice and unmistakable. But it also includes selections from various popular "authorities," as Tom Sawyer might put it, from abroad and at home, including the celebrated English hunting chronicler Henry William Herbert ("Frank Forester"), New York's C. W. Gooter, and Southerners ranging from the local Dr. Egbert B. Johnston of Tuskegee to Colonel William Stockton of Florida, himself known well to sporting readers under the pseudonym "Cor de Chasse."

This republication of *Dog and Gun* resolves the first problem, and more importantly, it also opens the way, through an opportunity to re-examine the other matters outlined above, toward new speculations about the text's ongoing appeal, interest, and importance, both to the scholar and the general reader. For, in a phrase intentionally invoking some old clichés, this work of barely more than a hundred pages—about the size of a popular farmer's almanac or agricultural manual—speaks not only volumes but worlds.

As a literary-social text, it speaks, for instance, the world of popular publishing in the mid-nineteenth century, including newspapers and agricultural pamphlets; magazines and "sporting journals" of immense popular appeal such as Porter's *Spirit of the Times*; and hardbound volumes of "sporting humor" such as those also described above, which, in the last days before the Civil War, briefly conjoined the worlds of North and South in literary community. It also stands among a host of instructional and special-interest texts in the long-accredited "how-to-do-it" tradition beginning with Benjamin Franklin and extending to the newest gentleman's digest or hunting-fishing magazine on this morning's rack. As with many of the same, it is a do-it-yourself text with distinct social implications. The book provides an established fraternity with the opportunity to peruse and savor in a codified, useful fashion, a certain kind of recreational technology that reassures it about the integ-

rity of its values and the permanence of its class status.   In
addition, like perhaps a modern golf or tennis guide, Hooper's volume provides an engagingly written, relatively inex-
pensive source of education in potential advancement, as
measured here by the ability to exhibit gentlemanly be-
havior in the hunting field (a point surely not lost on author
or audience in a work by the creator of the endlessly self-
promoting Suggs).

In sum, Hooper's *Dog and Gun* is a literary-cultural document in any number of dimensions of major, newly estimable
worth, speaking volumes about lost "worlds": about popular
publishing, about publishing commerce, about the types and
textures of pre–Civil War American regionalisms, about the
politics of Northern versus Southern life, urban versus
rural, industrial versus agricultural, commercial or working
versus landed or leisured professional.   It is about commerce and work, about land and leisure as social com-
modities, about whole orders of political and cultural value.

As a literary-cultural document of this sort, *Dog and Gun*
fulfills these claims to renewed importance, explicitly and
implicitly.   The volume speaks "worlds" in what it describes
by way of direct presentation: in the wealth of things it says
about a hunting culture amazingly like other contemporary
models of the gentry—Russian, French, German, and—
most decidedly—English.   Indeed, it would not be outlandish to describe *Dog and Gun* as Siegfried Sassoon without
the horses or Robert Graves without the public schools.
For here we have the full sense, albeit distinctively rendered against the landscape of a frequently rough-and-
tumble frontier, of a whole order of things in cultural eclipse
even as it struggles to achieve privileged codification.   We
have, for instance, the discrete defining of a particular kind
of leisure—on a particular kind of social-political landscape,
within a particular kind of "work" economy involving large
agricultural property ownership and profit, cheap, abundant

(and in many cases, slave) agricultural labor, and the proximity of large tracts of wilderness environment. Or, to use a more familiar analogy, Hooper describes the kind of world that still makes it necessary for a male visitor to the Black Belt to explain to certain audiences why he does not hunt in the sense that "hunting" of a very specific sort, with its specifically male rituals, humors, and decorums, continues to provide a major index of definition for a society invested in the dominance of a landed or professional gentry.

One can also look here, of course, to find the origins of broader types of Southern maleness, the good old boy, perhaps, as presented in the more "colorful" literary analogues of the period. For this is, clearly, a hunting culture in which it is accepted that every male hunts and does so invariably in accord with various cherished or deplored markings of class status. And in this respect it probably would be stretching a point to stress how far, on a rumbustious frontier, this volume would have appealed to the spirit of class mobility inspired by that rapscallion Suggs. (To be sure, *Dog and Gun* is, after all, a very "Franklin" kind of book, and one would at least like to imagine the raffish Suggs, reading avidly for future fun *and* profit in some newly planned impersonation.)

The tone here, however, is something less along the lines of envisioned class mobility and more along the lines of assumed class expectation. The basic attitude seems to be that what you see is what you get. A man who shoots as a gentleman will be assumed a gentleman, a person of nonquestionable antecedents. A person who shoots as a novice or a pot-hunter will be assumed a novice or a pot-hunter. Here, then, is a book meeting the specific needs of a society with something of the class bias of England, but now also with hunting established, whether for sport *or* subsistence, as an inalienable right of the citizens of nature's nation, the garden of the world, Southern division.

And it is exactly in this regional respect that cultural prophecy in *Dog and Gun* becomes complicated even further. For here we are also witness, almost as if it were this morning, to things most familiar. We envision—for instance, through frequent discussions centering on other hunting publications and on the particular details of gun and dog ownership—what will become major categories in a general commodification of leisure: both in the popular media, in artifacts as diverse as *Field and Stream* magazine, or in a syndicated fishing show; and in the "hard" domain of commodity, paraphernalia, appurtenances, the incredible commercial technologies in vehicles, weapons, tackle, equipment, now available on the mass market and purchased today by sportsmen at all levels of income. And now, also, at the old "upper" end of the spectrum, we recognize such commodification of leisure reintegrated with the gentlemanly kind of environmental citizenship encouraged by such organizations as Ducks Unlimited.

In sum, we find the constant mixings of upper-class sport with a macho, even a redneck appeal, but also the book's projection back into a peculiar kind of nature-ism that continues to define the hunting culture of the South. Then *and* now, this culture reveals a curious blend of appeals: it emphasizes the social naturalness of hunting, and also the naturalness of communing with nature, but without the metaphysical abstraction of Emerson; the naturalness of participation in natural process without the chaste asceticism of Thoreau; the assumption of hunting sportsmanship as a rightful extension of a particular kind of manly, domestic familiarity with firearms; and the equally rightful acceptance, born of enduring relationships with the land, of a natural necessity for the winnowing of wild populations (and here despite some appalling nineteenth-century numbers of slaughter and wastage) much more in the spirit of the traditional conservationist, as opposed to the more popularly deigned environmentalist.

The tone of the volume in all these respects is fairly set by the first paragraph of a first chapter entitled "The Gentleman's Amusement." It begins by explaining how two title-page epigraphs, one from the philosopher Ascham and the other from the poet Gay justify the author's claim of his subject, "Field Sports," as at once endowed with "manliness and innocence" and at the same time "not wanting in poetic dignity." Further appeal to authority invokes the name of a classic contemporary writer on the same subject, Henry William Herbert, Esq., author of the "unequalled *'Field Sports,'*" to whom the present work has already been lavishly dedicated. Finally, the "social" seriousness of the subject is underscored by attestation, gleaned of personal experience, from the author himself. "I need only add," he concludes, "that the shooting of game birds, over pointers and setters, has been, time out of mind, *the gentleman's* amusement; so much so, that I would hardly hesitate to make some guess concerning any man's antecedents, who should cross a stubble with me one of these crispy, brown October mornings."

At the same time, however, for all such assertions of social and literary control, it is also a disparate, miscellaneous book. It jumps along a line of chapters on technical subject after technical subject, including choice of weaponry and loading and charging; training of the setter and pointer; general advice to the sportsman; extended discussion, lavishly interspersed with anecdote and illustrative story, on the shooting of the quail, duck, woodcock, and partridge; and concluding chapters on treatment of the distemper and snipe shooting in Florida. And along the way, it does nothing to conceal that it is, as needed on its complicated collection of given topics, a treatise by many hands. Yet just in the teeming, diverse quality of the assembled lore (and often in a way reminiscent of the kind of padding-out familiar in Mark Twain's monster subscription volumes) lies a sense of its peculiar richness as a text of sundry authorities on various lost arts. If the book is in its way literary-seeming in its impressive preliminaries, epigraphs, dedications, and erudite references, and thus surely something worth having on the library shelf, it is at the same time endowed with a distinctly experiential and "working" flavor—something to keep with one's hunting gear and riding tack or to carry in the field. Moreover, it seems as well a timely, up to the minute book, often with notes and emendations recently added to materials obviously published first as newspaper copy. Overall, it gives the calculated impression of having come down to a literal footrace with the New York typesetters.

Above all, *Dog and Gun* is immensely full, as Mark Twain might have put it, of "Information." It tells us of diverse flora and fauna: fish, fowl, game animals, trees, plants, herbal and medicinal specifics, dogs, and horses. Its lessons and exempla involve technical authorities, local cognoscenti, gentleman sportsmen, "novices," and "pothunters." It covers types of weapons, both English and American, calibers, weights, prices, appropriate powders, types of shot. It specifies vocabulary, proper and improper, in issues of calling and naming, and, in some moments of technical complication, even tone of voice. It gives inside tips, lore vouchsafed by the experienced on the whip as opposed to the short halter as dog-training devices, or the relationship between powder load and weight of shot as to accuracy or killing power depending on the kind of game or hunting situation. Much of the information, even now, continues to be "informative" in a distinct quality of practical revelation of the particular kind of discipline that distinguishes the care, training, and general treatment of hunter breeds of dog from household pets, and thus by implication the rather different views on animal-human relationships held by those who work them for sport as opposed to those who cherish them for domestic-pastoral companionship. Much of it reminds us that hunting, no matter what the literary or class status of the person involved, is a willed participation in a fatal and, by many persons' definitions, cruel economy of nature.

On the other hand, much of the information now "comes back" also with a distinct appeal, at once charming and mournful, of matters distinctly antiquarian. Hooper tells us of species of fowl and fish, their attributes, their names technical, vernacular, and purely local, their place in the natural and the domestic economy. Some of the old information in this respect is distressing, for it includes the names of birds, fish, and other wildlife, now gone the way of the bear, the American bison, or, in tragic terminality, the passenger pigeon or the ivory-billed woodpecker. And the reasons are almost always there, by the numbers. For if one receives again, as in so many nineteenth-century texts, a sense of American nature's rife abundance, one also finds a dispiriting acceptance of common, casual slaughter. "A bag of fifty" is tossed off in an early note concerning a just-reported encounter by an east Alabama party with the relatively rare snipe. So, the toll of the Florida hunting expedition recorded in the final chapter is as follows: "one hundred twenty-four snipe, sixty-nine ducks, five brent, twenty-eight trout which will weigh over one hundred pounds." The local scorekeeper-commentator crows, "when this sport is exceeded, 'may we be there to see!'"

Of equal importance, as noted above, is the work's second dimension: its vision of the world that is also there *implicitly*, the world formed exactly in what it sometimes does not say or is now no longer able to say. It implies a whole economy of "nature," that is, exactly in its "civilized" be-

speaking of a whole economy of "culture," of common social
assumption, gesture, ritual, custom, observance.   Indeed,
although this must be reckoned a rural book, indelibly alive
is the whole world of "manners," a society's "hum and buzz
of implication."   Here, without much self-critical question-
ing, is a class society, and it is one in which the putatively
"upper" classes (modeled on the landowning English gentry
but including also the literate male professionals—lawyers,
doctors, journalists) mock and disdain their absent in-
feriors.   In the fashion of current historicist analysis, we
may also note by implication the assumed role in the culture
at large of certain marginalized groups here simply not
present and observe accordingly how the "presence" of their
"absence" speaks of economic and class relationships.
There is one woman in the whole narrative fabric, for instance, and she is reserved for the role of victim in a classic
sporting *cum* shaggy-dog anecdote in the long tradition of
the Southwestern practical joke.   Further, the book con-
tains but a single, even more evanescent mention of slaves,
identified as "negroes" in remarks on the much-deplored
practice of netting quail.   This book is simply about areas of
life in which the politics of domestic gender relation or of
the "peculiar institution" of slavery become issues precisely
to the degree that they remain uninscribed.

On a closer point of eloquently American absences or si-
lences, one is further astounded at how utterly "English" is
the hunting culture of the gentry, with its conventions, decorums, ground rules, its fussy enshrinements of the seemingly most technical details of attitude and ritual.   Gentlemen inform themselves about and practice the fine points of
weapons maintenance and dog and horse training, endowing
them with an almost religious codification, not only because
that is what well-bred and well-placed men do, but also because that is what their time is for.   Conversely, the book
implies that these gentlemen hunters for sport do not in any

way hunt for food or *act* like people who hunt for food precisely because "pot-hunting" is not what their time is for. Often they admit that they eat some or all of what they hunt. But they also insist, immediate matters of nourishment aside, that they would in any circumstances employ rules of sport that clearly encumber the work of mere food-getting. It is, as one would say now, "a status thing," and one so deeply ingrained in the character as to dictate silently the national vernacular to this day. The opposites of true knights of the field are "pot-hunting vagabonds" beyond the reach of "sportsmanship, humanity, and magnanimity" (60); and at the level of animal training, this translates correspondingly into the distinction between the "perfectly well-broken pointer and 'a pot-hunting cur'" (44–45). In short, we may newly remember what a "pot-shot" really is, and why, in the most abrupt terms of social condescension, a "sitting duck" is a sitting duck. Somewhere between a lost world and our own current hubbub and bustle, then, the language of the tribe continues to carry its own built-in level of civilization index, as it does in so many other ways we are not aware.

As to the particular scale on which "civilization" is measured, how tremendously English this book is can hardly be overestimated. In almost tragic pre-Civil War ways are compounded both the arrogance and innocence of cultural chauvinism that remind us of English pre-World War I memoirs in particular. We note, for instance, how English is the commerce, the preference for English guns, English powder, English shot, English wadding, English cleaning materials, English dogs, not to mention English authority on virtually any hunting subject worthy of discussion. Mobile is remarked on as the chief port of entry and most convenient site of sale for English goods.

On the other side, one notes the narrator's disdain for American manufactures. The finest rifles, for which the gentleman should reasonably expect to pay $300 to $500 without much whimper, can only be English. (Perhaps, in the most extreme financial emergency, certain houses in New York or Philadelphia might serve to fill the unfortunate void.) And equally pronounced is the narrator's reluctance to esteem American work in what might be called more general ordnance technologies: his dubiousness about certain new forms of bore and barrel construction; his outright refusal to use anything but English powder. In sum, one finds something like gentlemanly or even cavalier contempt for the industrial, technological plant north of the Mason-Dixon line. In matters of precision engineering and massed technologies, one senses already the crude, accumulated might of Northern ordnance. Hooper provides one last "sporting" look, as it were, at the South's gross misconception of Anglo-American and Northern-Southern trade relations, industries, and technologies, here focused in a crucial area of precision weapons production that would prove literally fatal.

Finally, one cannot leave cultural analysis without reminding the reader how tremendously "literary" a book *Dog and Gun* is as well. And given the author's status as a journalist, a good part of such literariness comes here both of Hooper's own making and also of his discerning, literary-editorial eye. In anecdote, instruction, appeal to authority, the text frequently juxtaposes English and American "hunting" classics unparalleled in quality and in comparative richness of stylistic distinction and particularity. There is Jenner on inoculation; "'Dinks on Dogs;'" Dr. E. B. J. of Macon County on field training. Two longer, late narratives in this comparative vein especially strike the eye and the spirit.

First, two companion pieces entitled "My First Day's Partridge Shooting" and "The Yorkshire Moors" are adduced from the incomparable Englishman, Herbert, to recall a boy's introduction to the gentlemanly art, and a vista of the fine English hunting landscape set out against the glorious twelfth of August. Interwoven with the narrative of the young Etonian initiated into the mysteries of manly discipline and camaraderie, we have the vision of a whole universe, frozen in the rich, autumnal, burnished style of nineteenth-century England. And how truly "centered" a vision it all seems, sure in its diction, syntax, paragraphing, overall design; its opening, elaboration, closure; its sense of a single "story" that is at once the "story" of a time and a world and of a certain way of looking at the world, bespeaking an irreplaceable completeness of cultural authority.

Yet then, equally brilliant in its way, is the American counterpart that follows shortly, "Snipe Shooting in Florida," by Col. Wm. T. Stockton, popularly known in the hunting papers as "Cor de Chasse." For it is also at once a masterpiece, just in its particularly *de*-centered way, of both American "nature" writing in the vein of Bartram or Audubon, and of American "humorous" writing rendered through the robust narrative theatricalities of the Old Southwest. In contrast to Herbert, there is the exaggerated mixing of elevated and vernacular styles, somehow like a language-current persistently shot between two contending poles of decorum. Certain "shooting-grounds," for instance, "afford full feed to the Brent, Black duck, Mallard, Grey duck, Teal, *et id omne genus*. The highlands around the lake are crowned with handsome residences, and the youthful sportsman may almost hope that his skill is looked upon and admired by ladies fair, even should they fail to recognise him on account of the sepia tinge he may have acquired from a plunge into an alligator bed, or some similar 'causa teterrima *belli*,' anglice, going *almost* waist deep into a mud hole" (98).

As with the astonished "passing countryman" on the site who has just witnessed some of the narrator's fancy shoot-

ing, to such lavish display one can only respond "I tell *you*!"
Like the America it represents, the style of hunting narrative here seems to be going nearly every place at once.
And so throughout, as in so much of the expression of the
Old Southwest, literary-rhetorical tricks, tropes, and flour-
ishes providing the signature of a distinctive educational and
class status mingle with outlandish local flavor and detail.
A black cook named Sam serves up Snipe *en papillote*
(102). The sated sportsmen smoke "the *post-cœnal* cigar"
(103). A sturdy nightcap, followed by several more "smiles"
as they are daintily described, results for one of the party in
"a throe (throw?) of nature" quickly blamed by the overin-
dulging party on "'Those d——d snipe!'" (104). Meanwhile,
the narrator smothers his hilarity amidst the blankets, not-
ing, "All that sympathy *could* do was to control the risibles"
(104). Again, it is the standard American mixture of wry
circumlocutions and wanton common-nesses, rejoicing at
once in sublimities and beauties, pratfalls and discomforts.
And so likewise in contrast to Herbert's English certainties
and straightforwardness of development, this American
hunting fable proceeds along its own distinctive meander-
ings, and like so many of its indigenous narrative kin, by
digressions, incidental observations, "factual" insertions, in-
terpolations of opinion, technical and political. It seems almost to rejoice in narrative mixings and discontinuities, ab-
surd abridgments, hiatuses, and leaps, stories so filled with
stories upon stories upon stories that one eventually wonders which was the one in the first place that seemed all
that important.

This quality of literary *cum* roughneck genius in *Dog and
Gun* must also lead us back to a final note on "literariness"
in a text that often presents Hooper himself at his familiar
best. To be sure, even as "hunting literature" of a certain
sort, it is surely not Irving, Turgenev, Sassoon, or Heming-
way—literature, that is, of a "hunting" culture, having as

its main function the distinctly "literary" evocation of a world or a code. *Dog and Gun* is, and was meant to be, mainly a manual. But it is a manual by a writer who could not even write technical narrative without endowing it with a certain peculiar character of literary genius.

The opening pages, as noted earlier, are nothing less than the charting of a world, a literary style that is a social politic. It is also a highly personal, and in the sense of an old, good, serviceable term, characteristic literary style. Wry, periphrastic, thoroughly at home in the world, it is the style of a peculiarly American kind of "confidence." It is at once the "confidence" of a Simon Suggs in all the arts by which men "get along" in the world; but here it is also the "confidence" of a gentleman authoritatively detailing his sense of the importance of certain gentlemanly pursuits in their connections with important cultural values not at all likely to be disturbed by the occasional charlatan or interloper.

Throughout, there is the satirical humor of class commentary coupled with the gentlemanly humor of polite, albeit generally off-color raillery. There is even, as surely could not be helped in a book by Johnson J. Hooper, at least one major practical joke. Not surprisingly, it is a joke directed at a woman. And it is, of course, coarse. It begins in this vein with the woman herself who is clearly, besides being "decidedly *fast* for her age," conspicuously overweight. ("God bless her!" the narrator intones in a gallant parenthesis; "may her shadow never grow less!") A woman of decided appetites, she has developed in "Gotham," it turns out, a fondness for "the game birds of the North—Woodcock in particular" (71). The narrator, loath to deny her wants, decides to supply the nearest substitute from the local regions, which is clearly that kind of woodcock more familiarly known (although never quite named here, in a book often insistent on accurate naming) as woodpecker. He then persuades her to have it prepared, planning at the last minute to reveal the joke before any of the offending portion is consumed. Unfortunately, he is called away on the night of the planned supper. As a result, in the presence of a table full of reluctant, queasy fellow diners, the culinary part of the experiment actually occurs: "The epicurean lady ate it with a decided *gusto*;—rich, rare and spicy were her plaudits of the game bird, the peculiar *game* flavor, &c. But enough; the joke was really carried farther than I intended, and I am sorry for it, as my fair friend cannot bear a game bird to this day" (72–73). Here is Hooper unmistakably, the game bird in his game book, laughing and crowing like the Southern woodcock, who is in fact probably a woodpecker in disguise with a raucously high opinion of himself and a raucously low sense of what is funny.

Like his book, Hooper is somehow vulgar, reticent, hilarious, cruel, and polite. And here, as the literary Hooper, he steps forward stage center as the literary genius of a hunting manual written, we now see, by an author himself the member of a colorful, raucous, endangered species. He is in a moment the Southwestern Gentleman-Humorist and the Humorist-Gentleman, both a new mutation for hard weather and an evolutionary throwback in his literary-cultural economy, a vivid natural curiosity yet something necessarily sacrificed to history in the name of progress. Here, again, *Dog and Gun* allows us to remember something lost, and it further challenges us to seek out the memory of many of those things, dark questions, social issues, about which it lamentably fails to speak. Moreover, what it does not tell us, we must continue to insist, includes important things we cannot afford, for good or ill, to allow to lie forgotten. Yet still, the past in its fullness of good *and* ill is the only past that can be ours to recover. And for just that reason, in books such as *Dog and Gun*, we can still take heart from a time when the world, and we in it, for good and ill, were somehow at once both older and younger.

Apace, we go back in years and seasons to the autumnal ritual of the hunt, where one is always a greenhorn with a first gun and an old, chastened veteran of one of the oldest of earth's mysteries. The book presents the natural mystery of quest, competition, predation, pursuit, survival, bravery, endurance, and eventual death. Its hunting culture is as old and otherworldly as legend, and, for persons in this region, as familiar as Faulkner, as close as a cornfield in Clay County or a deer woods in the Black Belt. Or, as the first page of Hooper's book puts it, and as echoed in the old familiar song, it is someplace in the South where it is autumn again, somewhere early on a frosty morning. For the ongoing tradition of literary-cultural memory of which *Dog and Gun* now again becomes a part, old times there are not forgotten.

Dog and Gun

DEDICATION.

TO HENRY WILLIAM HERBERT, ESQ.,

"THE CEDARS," NEW JERSEY.

DEAR SIR: Knowing you only through your works, I take the liberty of inscribing to you these "*Loose Chapters*," on a subject which your own pen has so fully adorned, conscious that the chief merit in them is to be found in those portions which you, and other "shooting" friends, have contributed to them. If this little book incites the young Sportsman to read your own unequalled "*Field Sports*," it will have accomplished its main purpose.

Respectfully,

Your obedient Servant,

THE AUTHOR.

DOG AND GUN;

A Few Loose Chapters on Shooting.

AMONG WHICH WILL BE FOUND

SOME ANECDOTES AND INCIDENTS.

BY JOHNSON J. HOOPER,

OF MONTGOMERY, ALA.

"And I promise you *shootinge*, by my judgment, is the most honeste pastime of all, and suche one, I am sure, of all other, that hindereth learninge litel or notninge at all, whatsoever you and some other saye "—ASCHAM—*Old English Writer*

> See how the well-taught pointer leads the way ;
> The scent grows warm ; he stops ; he springs the prey ;
> The fluttering covey from the stubble rise,
> And on swift wing divide the sounding skies !"
> [GAY—*Rural Sports*

NEW YORK:

ORANGE JUDD & COMPANY,

AGRICULTURAL BOOK PUBLISHERS,

41 PARK ROW.

DOG AND GUN.

CHAPTER I.

THE GENTLEMAN'S AMUSEMENT.

MY young sporting friends will observe, that in my title I fortify my own opinion of the manliness and innocence of Field Sports with a classic authority, while the quotation from the bard, shows our theme not wanting in poetic dignity. In my day I have heard the delightful pastime much reviled by prejudiced ignorance and under-bred and over-done morality; but while the advocate of Dog and Gun is backed by old *Ascham*, and a host of such ancient worthies, and finds among the writers of the present day such aid as is afforded by the graphic and versatile pen of HERBERT, he may well afford to treat all cavillers, high or low, with a quiet curl of his lip. I need only add. that the shooting of game birds, over pointers and setters, has been, time out of mind, *the gentleman's* amusement; so much so, that I would hardly hesitate to make some guess concerning any man's antecedents, who should cross a stubble with me one of these crispy, brown October mornings.

Getting towards the main topic as speedily as possible, I will remark in a general way that, in this region, game proper may be considered as limited to the Quail and two or three varieties of Duck. Both Woodcock and Snipe,

though increasing latterly, have been too sparsely scattered
through Eastern Alabama, to be worthy of particular attention. Here and there, there are some few grounds, in the
neighborhood of large streams, where a day's sport may
be had, at the proper season, shooting the latter. It is
likely, however, judging by the past, that in a few years
both will afford fine amusement to the Alabama sportsman.*
At present, I suspect that my friends, Col. Augustus Brooks
and A. R. Meslier, Esq., bag more snipe and cock, in the
immediate neighborhood of Mobile, than are killed in all
the rest of the State put together. If, in this idea, I am
mistaken, I shall be very much obliged to any friend who
can furnish me an authoritative correction. Indeed, in
all that I write on the subject of sporting, I would have it
remembered I bring a very limited experience to bear;
and I fulfil a promise made, some time ago, to several
young friends, as much to direct their attention to the
works of *Frank Forester* (Herbert), *Hawker* (Am. Ed.
by W. T. Porter, Esq.), " *Dinks*," and others, as to con-
vey a few grains of information suitable to this latitude, and
not perhaps to be readily picked up in sporting books.

It may be added, that whoso takes the *Spirit of the
Times* will find that, from week to week, during the appropriate seasons, Mr. Porter's correspondents furnish abund-

---

⁰ Since the foregoing paragraph first appeared in print, I have
been informed by my friend, H. C. S., Esq., of Montgomery, that
as fine snipe-shooting as the world affords may be had, in the proper season, in the prairies south of Montgomery. In " the bend" of
the Alabama, opposite the city, also, I am informed, that a bag of
fifty may sometimes be secured by a good shot. Perhaps before I
have done with the series, some friend will furnish a " full, true
and particular" account of the best localities for the bird, and the
mode of shooting them. As I understand it now, dogs are not used.
While on the subject of *snipe*, I may remark that the writer flushed
and shot a solitary bird, on the 23d Dec. ult., on the edge of a duck-
pond, not very far from Montgomery. He was an excellent case.

ance of facts, feats, and general information in the sporting
line, a great deal of which is really valuable, as throwing
light on the history and habits of the game of the country.

To return from a digression : The *Quail* is our chief,
most reliable game bird in this section. A brave fellow he
is too, and worthy to be properly known and called by
his own true name, and not by his universal misnomer,
Partridge. Let all true sportsmen call him aright—leaving
it to the pot-hunter who shoots the bevy as it huddles on
the ground, or murders the whistling cock on the fence or
stump, and the clown who nets or traps what he cannot
fairly kill, to apply to him a name for which there is no
owner on this continent. Every one who writes on sports
of the field has his rules; and *my* RULE THE FIRST is—
Call Quail, QUAIL! Persistently give him his true name,
and you are, young reader, one step nearer sportsmanship
than the *commune vulgus* who kill him foully and serve
him *more* foully, to wit: in hog's lard. Presently I shall
tell you what I know of the habits of the bird, and when
you have added your own observation thereunto, you will
quite probably attain to killing him in good style, and to
knowing how to have him dressed with a half-teaspoonful
of pale brandy, permeated through his plump breast, according to the recipe of my friend, Dr. E. B. J., of Macon.

Of the ducks that visit us here (except the *Canvas-
back*, and some other varieties in Mobile Bay, about
which I know nothing, but of which I should like to receive information from those who do), incomparably the
finest is that old stand-by, the *Mallard.* Shot, or only *to
be* shot, he is *the* duck of our waters ; whereby, I mean
that the sport he affords, on the river or the table, is superior to that we derive from any of the genus *Anas.* Next
to him, the *Blue-winged Teal* is considered generally to
rank. Then comes the Wood or Summer Duck, known
generally in the country as the *Striped-head.* There are

a few other species, less common, that I may refer to hereafter.

I have mentioned now the different varieties of game about which, as it respects their habits and the modes of killing, I propose to write, in these discursive essays. As I go along, I hope to get aid from more experienced persons ; and I especially ask it from those who have signified a willingness to contribute to the *Mail** on the subject of *Sporting*.

It will be well enough to close this chapter with some remarks on

SPORTING TERMS.

It may be here observed, that there is more than appears, at first blush, in uniformity of sporting nomenclature. Without looking at all to the fact, that the sportsman's associations leak out by the terms of art which he uses, just as the ill-bred fellow is detected by the ordinary dialect he affects, it is desirable that persons pursuing field-sports, in any given section of country, should adopt the same phraseology, for reasons growing out of the *positive inconvenience* of want of uniformity.   To illustrate : A has been accustomed all his life to the use of the proper word, *toho !* to bring his dog to a stand.   He can no more —in ninety instances out of the hundred—bring himself to substitute the word *heed !* when a-field, than he can fly. But he gets a dog broken by some ignorant trainer, which has been taught to obey this slang word of command ; and by the end of the week, he has *Dash* thoroughly confused between *toho !* and *heed !*—and himself just about as much so.   Or, B lends a young dog (broken to the slang word), to a friend, because he knows that friend is an accomplished sportsman, for a day's shooting.   The

* A newspaper published at Montgomary, Ala., by the author.

friend discovers that *Plato* is rather eagerly pressing a
running bevy, and with regulated, steady voice, not loud,
gives the order, *toho!* *Plato* is probably expecting the
word he was taught, and hearing it not, but another in its
stead, springs in and flushes—and, possibly, runs a quarter of a mile before he can be brought in. The friend
trounces him severely, the dog the while only vaguely conscious of a fault—for his mind is not carried back to the
disobeying of a command he was previously taught to
obey. There you have it: the shooter curses the dog for
an ill-taught mongrel (when he is, perhaps, a capital
young pointer, only a trifle heady), and sets him back in
his education, by allowing him to flush and by the whip-
ping, fully half a season. To illustrate again : you might
as well break *horses* as *dogs* to diverse words of command.
Add to all this, the convenience to those who interchange
opinions, theories, experiences, on the subject of shooting,
through the press, or conversationally, and I think the
argument becomes irresistible in favor of *a Uniform
Sporting Nomenclature.*

Mr. Herbert's work on Field Sports is the standard in
this country, on this and cognate subjects. I quote from
it, as many of the technical terms of the art as are necessary for the range I propose to cover :

QUAIL, a single hatching	A BEVY.
SNIPE, " " . . .	A BROOD.
WOODCOCK, " "	A BROOD.
QUAIL, several hatchings together .	A PACK.
QUAIL, less than grown, are . .	SQUEAKERS.
SNIPE, flocking together, are . .	A WHISP.
WILD DUCK, a large flock, is . . .	A TEAM.
WILD DUCK, a small flock, is . .	A PLUMP.
TEAL, a number is	A FLOCK.
TWO QUAIL, make	A BRACE.
" WOODCOCK, " SNIPE, or } make . . .	A COUPLE. " DUCKS,

Two Pointers or Setters, are	.	A Brace.
Three " "	. . .	A Leash.
To make a Bird Dog stand	. . .	Toho !

"	"	drop to shot	. .	Charge !
"	"	come behind	.	Heel !
"	"	move cautiously		Steady !
"	"	rise from the charge		Hold Up !
"	"	hunt for dead bird	.	Seek Dead !
"	"	bring in dead after pointing it	. .	Fetch !

Having given thus much from Herbert's *Sporting Nomenclature*, I may add that a dog is said to *quarter his ground*, NOT "to hunt about the field;" he *breaks his charge*, and does *not* "jump up and run after the birds." He *retrieves* game when he brings it in. He *flushes the bevy* (if he is ill-behaved,) and does not "scare up the flock." The single bird sometimes *towers*, (*i. e.* flies very high and almost perpendicularly), if shot through the brain or heart. The bevy generally *flies to covert* when disturbed, but the sportsman *marks them down*. If he is a good shot, he *bags* quite a number.

My young readers will remember my *Rule the First : Call Quail*, Quail !

And here I will add another almost as short. It is founded on the fact that there is no such thing as a *Partridge*, on the whole broad continent—a fact that taboos to the American sportsman the word *corey*. I know that far better sportsmen than I am, habitually use it ; but it is a custom we should "reform altogether." My *Rule the Second*, then, is : *Call a Bevy of Quail*, A Bevy of Quail !

CHAPTER II.

HOW TO CHOOSE A GOOD GUN.

THE prime necessity of a young sportsman, is, of course, a GOOD GUN. If he has plenty of money, there need be little difficulty in supplying himself, quite speedily, with an excellent article. He has but to get a friend, or some reliable business man, not in the trade of selling guns, to import him one from the workshop of Westley Richards, or Purday, or Moore, or some other crack English maker, and the thing is done. Such a gun, reliable and perfectly well-finished, will cost from $300 to $500 Frank Forester tells us that guns, a good deal resembling this fine English work (and really being of English manufacture), put up in very nice mahogany cases, with velvet lining, may be bought for from $75 to $150. Hundreds of these guns are sold annually, in hardware and other stores. They are called by Forester *Brumagem* ware, taking the name from a corruption of *Birmingham* (England), where a vast deal of such showy but unreliable stuff is fabricated. By the way, Richards is the only Birmingham maker of any repute, and it is said of him, in these latter days, that his barrels are too soft. At any rate, his reputation is on the decline. Manton (the successor, of course, of old Joe Manton), is a fourth rate maker. There are a dozen or more, however, who are said to make as good guns as "old Joe" ever did, and there is no difficulty in getting the article, provided you are able and willing to pay for it; but the best informed think it bad policy to import a gun which costs under

$300. Even that is rather low. If unable to stand these figures, the better plan, according to Herbert, is to get Constable, of Philadelphia, or John Mullin, of 16 Ann street, New York, to build you one. Of the former, I know nothing, except by reputation ; but of Mr. Mullin I can speak, after trying his work, with the utmost confidence. He built me a gun, a little more than a year ago, at the instance of my friend, Mr. Porter, of the *Spirit of the Times*, which comes up fully to all he engaged it should do. I believe that his *forte* is the making of the heavier descriptions of barrels, especially for bay and river duck-shooting. His work is perfectly neat, and while, of course, it wants the extreme finish of the costly English gun, is to the full as honest a shooter. And if for $150 (with $10 to $20 for cover, case, and small appliances), you get a piece with all the substantial qualities of *hard, close shooting, regularity in dispersion of shot*, and *aurability of barrels and locks*, which you would obtain in an English gun for $300 or $400, the gain is greatly yours. These qualities I and some friends of mine have obtained, within these last two or three years, from Mr. Mullin, at the mentioned price. The guns he has sent to Georgia and Alabama, so far as I can ascertain, after a good deal of inquiry, have in no instance failed to prove themselves the very hardest and closest shooters.

While on the subject of Mullin's work, I will state that his best barrels are *laminated steel*. Somehow or other, I had imbibed a strong prejudice against them, notwithstanding one of the very best guns I ever shot was one of them, made by Stevens, which I have parted with because it *was* of laminated steel. It was a little difficult for Mr. Mullin to convert me from this prejudice, but he did finally succeed. In a letter to me, he says : " I give you a description of the laminated steel barrels, which *you seem so much to fear*. They are made of thin layers of steel, twisted as a rope of three strands, and then twisted around a rod to form the barrel ; then welded and then put through the annealing process, which takes all, or nearly all, of the *carbon* out, and leaves the barrels all the *closeness* of steel, and all the *toughness* of fine iron. Suppose all the carbon is taken out of your razor, and it rendered iron once more, then what iron can compare with it in closeness and toughness ?"   Again, in another letter, he sends me a *table of the comparative capacity of resistance* of different barrels, and says : " I hope the scale opposite will satisfy your fears, and when you come to use the gun, I feel certain no man could prevail on you to go back to iron barrels; the steel *kill* so clean and *keep* so clean, and no give-out in their shooting powers."   Again he says : " They (the steel barrels) will not *lead* on account of their closeness, nor *breech-burn*, but maintain their power of shooting," &c.

The following is the table of comparative strength of the different materials used in gun building, furnished me a year or two since by Mr. Mullin :

		PRESSURE OF THE CHARGE.	SURPLUS STRENGTH.
Laminated Steel is equal to a pressure of . .	6,022 lbs.	1,700 lbs.	4,322 lbs.
Stubb Twist	4,818 "	"	3,118 "
Charcoal Iron	4,526 "	"	2,826 "
Three-penny Skelp Iron	3,841 "	"	2,141 "
Damascus Iron	3,292 "	"	1,592 "
Two-penny Skelp Iron .	2,840 "	"	1,140 "

Assuming the correctness of this comparison, and I know nothing to throw any doubt upon it, the laminated steel ought to drive other descriptions of barrels out of the market entirely. The "two-penny skelp " guns, I presume, are those which we see sold every day, in the stores, painted outside in rings like a raccoon's tail, and which are familiarly known as pot-metal. How any man of sense should risk his life forty times a day with such a weapon, I cannot comprehend; but I presume a great many who have brains do not so jeopard them.

In determining as to the size of a gun, reference is of course to be had to the character of the shooting it is intended for Practically, in the South, almost every man limits himself to a single gun "of all work." He wants one convenient and tolerably effective in a deer, turkey, or duck hunt, and not too heavy for a day's fagging after quail or snipe. All writers and persons of any experience, agree that the dimensions of a gun for these various purposes, are as follows :—

Length of barrels,	. .	32 inches.
Gauge,	. . . .	No. 14.
Weight,	. . .	$6\frac{1}{2}$ to $7\frac{1}{2}$ lbs.

I believe that, from some cause, or other, more *good* guns are made of these measurements than of any other. It may be that the makers have so many to supply, that practice and experience in the particular size have gradually taught the exact relations of all the parts.

For the larger game mentioned above, it is better to have 32 to 34 inches, 10, 11, or 12 gauge, and 8 to 9 lbs. weight. But most men overweight themselves. A gun should be fully within the strength of the person who is to handle it. A strong man, *ceteris paribus*, shoots always better than a feeble one; the weak should shoot as light guns as are effective. To be sure, I do not practice what I preach-shooting an eight and a half pound gun, when six pounds would better suit my muscles—but then all small men are ambitious!

The custom of using long, small-gauged guns—for instance (and nothing is more common), barrels 34 to 36 inches, and 15 to 18 guage—is ridiculous. No man but a pot-hunter, ignorant and irreclaimable, would do so. Not but that many of these guns do shoot excellently, but they do so not on account of their great length. In my opinion, a 14 gauge gun of 32 inches will carry as far as the same gauge with a half dozen inches added. If you increase the calibre, length may properly be added; but for any shoulder gun, I have no doubt 34 inches is quite enough, though possibly two inches more may benefit.

In purchasing guns in New York, or importing them to that city, I would recommend any friend of mine to engage the services of no one, out of the trade, but Wm. T. Porter, Esq., of the *Spirit of the Times*. If he has one *made* there, let him by all means go to Mullin, whom I recommend simply and solely, because I have dealt with him, paid him his best prices and got just what I wanted on all occasions.

Having got a gun, we naturally proceed to charge it. The chief difficulty is to obtain clean, strong powder. I know of but one powder answering this description*— that of Curtis & Harvey, English manufacturers. Their diamond grain is all that powder can be, or ought to be; their large grain, ducking powder, does not answer so well for *our* river and pond duck shooting. My attention was first attracted to the Diamond Grain by Forester's work, and I have never since willingly used any other. It is rather stronger than Du Pont's, and a pound will hardly foul a gun so much as a half dozen loads of the latter, which, like all American powder, is ineffably filthy. Curtis & Harvey's powder can generally be obtained of Messrs. W. B. & A. R. Bell, Dry Goods Dealers, Montgomery, and of Aubrey & Co., Produce Merchants, Mobile. These firms

---

* Since the above was written, I have become satisfied that the " *Electric Powder*," of the *Hazard Company*, is almost as clean as the " Diamond Grain." It is *the best* Aerican Powder. Parker, Morris & Co , of Mobile, are the Agents for Alabama.

import it, principally as an accommodation to their sporting friends, and sell it at $1 25—low enough, all things
considered.

For caps, Starkey has the best reputation, but his are
excessively dear. Eley's double water proof, at $3 a
thousand, are good enough for anybody. Richards' are
said to be good. I know no others that are,

As for cartridges, Eley's are the only ones. They are
excellent for a careful, good shot, and increase the effective
range of a gun from 20 to 40 yards. But careless or in-
expert hands will find no advantage in them; the reason is
at moderate distances they require an exactitude of aim
very nearly the same as in rifle shooting. I shall say
more of them hereafter.

CHAPTER III.

ON THE CHARGING OF A GUN.

IT may seem almost a waste of time, ink and paper, to discourse at any considerable length, of so simple a matter as the *charging of a gun*. And yet, I feel certain, that ignorance on this subject is more general than on almost any other branch of sporting. The number of men who load properly, is exceedingly small in proportion to the number who shoot. There are errors very common, both as to the proportions of powder and shot, and as to the comparative effect of light and heavy charges.

Pot-hunters invariably load by far too heavily. Observe boys who hunt squirrels and birds about the outskirts of the town, and you will soon see that any one of them will consume, in an afternoon, about as much ammunition as would serve a sportsman for a whole day's continuous shooting. The vulgar idea is, that a shot-gun is effective in proportion to the amount of powder and lead crammed down it, and many do therefore procure very large guns because they will bear larger crammings—and that without much reference to the particular service in which the piece is to be employed. All popular fallacies have *some slight* foundation in fact; but that reasoning which says, that if one and a quarter drachms powder and one ounce shot will, with a particular gun, kill quail at forty yards, *double the quantity* of each will kill the same bird at eighty yards, is utterly defective.

There is hardly a better test of sportsmanship than a man's mode of loading his gun. It is true that one *may*

load well and shoot badly, but practically it will be found
to be very rarely the case. The doing of this thing well
implies the powers of observation which go far towards
making a passably good shot. Possibly a deficiency of a
physical nature, such as want of muscle or unsteadiness
of nerve, may unfortunately belong to the individual who
charges his gun in the very best manner; but then he
knows how the shooting ought to be done.

As I have said already, most guns are overloaded.
There is usually about as great a quantity of powder
burned in shooting squirrels, at twenty to forty yards,
as it would be proper to expend in shooting deer, or
even bear, at long ranges. It is really a wonder that
more of the pot-metal barrels do not burst under the treatment they receive, in this respect. Their owners pack
them with a liberality which can only be the result of
absolute ignorance of the powers of the agencies they
invoke. A half-handful of powder and a handful of
shot is about the common charge, without any considera-
tion as to distance, size of shot, kind of game, or capacity
of the gun.

The little experience I have had, leads me to the be-
lief, that even with good sportsmen, the error is almost
invariably *overcharging*. In shooting quail, particularly,
very small loads are sufficient. One of the most successful of my friends shoots a little less than a drachm of powder
to about three-quarter ounce of number-seven shot. With
this charge he is quite as certain at long shots, as any
one of my acquaintance. I think, however, that he is a
little under the mark as to quantity of powder, and uses
shot a number too large. For quail shooting, the true proportions, in my opinion, are :

Powder ("Diamond Grain,") one and a half drachm.

Shot, number eight, one ounce.

This I would give only as an approximation to the true

proportions for the thirty-two inch fourteen-gauge gun; because the peculiar shooting of the particular gun may make some slight change necessary. For instance, a very strong shooter will not need more than a drachm to make the ounce of shot thoroughly effective at any ordinary range. Again, though number eight, "day in and day out," is—as Forester stoutly maintains—*the* shot for quail, yet I have known guns which killed them cleverly with sevens which *did not* do so with eights.

The reason for which eights are preferred is that the number of pellets to the ounce is much larger than of sevens. The difference between these two numbers is greater than between any other two numbers of shot. Forester estimates that a number-eight shot bears the same relation, in size, to a quail, that a grape shot does to a man of ordinary frame. Allowing, then, largely for superior tenacity of life, on the part of the bird, the smaller shot is amply large for his execution, *if driven through him*, as it always will be, if the gun is of the right kind and properly charged.

For snipe shooting, I suppose that there need be no variation from the above, except as to the size of shot. Most persons use *nines*, I believe, in this kind of shooting. My experience does not entitle me to an opinion, but if I ever have opportunity to try the sport, I shall experiment with a number smaller—number ten.

Perhaps the widest variances, in so far as shot are concerned, occur among those who shoot ducks. Those who depend mainly on killing them on the water, from behind a stump or log, invariably use large shot—from threes up to B. Those who do not go a-pot hunting use fours and fives, and some as low as sixes. The last mentioned is, however, quite *small enough* for the *Mallard*, which is remarkably strong both of bone and feather. They will not only carry off, at times, a good many pellets, but their strong plumage is excellently defensive against shot. Coming breast on in a right line, it is commonly believed that the thick cushion of feathers on the body will cause small shot to deflect. But I am inclined to think that a difference of one or even two numbers would not change the effect, in this respect.

Forester recommends number four for the Mallard, and I would sooner stand on his than any other single experience. For such guns as are most commonly used in the sport, the correct charge would be about

One and three-quarter drachms powder.

One and a quarter ounce shot.

These are less than the quantities spoken of in the Sporting Books, in connection with the subject of Duck Shooting; but it must be borne in mind that I always speak, in these papers, with reference to guns of a maximum weight of nine pounds.

For *Turkey Shooting*, the most successful hunters I know, recommend B or BB shot. The old-fashioned idea of large buckshot is going out of vogue. The turkey has immense vitality, and it really makes little difference with what size of shot you blow a hole through his body, if you leave his back, wings and legs unbroken : he will be very apt to take himself off, out of your reach, to die. *For riddling the head and neck* (which can be done at forty to fifty yards with any good gun), the chances are very greatly multiplied by the use of B or BB shot; and either of these sizes will very effectually break a wing or disable the back. As a general thing, in all sorts of shooting, the most common mistake is to use too large pellets ; but the disadvantages of doing so are hardly as manifest in any other description of hunting, as in turkey shooting.

I have no doubt but that Eley's Wire Cartridge answers a better purpose for killing the turkey, than for any other game. The sport generally gives ample time for careful shooting, and the great force of the cartridge and its regular dispersion of shot, enable the hunter to count with great certainty on perforating the neck or head, at fifty or even sixty yards. But in shooting cartridges, there is a rule to be remembered which does not hold, at all in the shooting of loose shot. With the latter, the less the powder used, the closer your shot go. With the cartridge, the greater the charge of powder, *the greater the velocity* of the cartridge, and, consequently, the less the time allowed, in a given distance, for the expulsion of the shot from the wire cage, and the consequent scattering. You must therefore increase your powder (up to a certain limit, of course), to increase the velocity of the cage and its contents. If I were going to shoot turkeys, I would use two drachms of moderately coarse-grained powder to an ounce and a half of B shot. Or two and a half drachms powder to a BB cartridge.

This suggests to my mind the chief objection I have to Eley's cartridge. The BB cartridge, gauge 11, weighs two ounces; *i. e.* one and a half ounce shot, and half ounce bone dust (in alternate layers with the shot), wire cage, cork, and paper. These two ounces are in a very dense, compact form ; it is almost equivalent to shooting the same quantity of bar lead. The weight requires at least two and a half drachms strong powder to keep it well in line for fifty-five or sixty yards. If it was made to weigh half an ounce less, its range would, I think, be considerably increased by the use of the same amount of powder. Very few men like to shoot more than two and a half drachms, and some will not go that far. A reduction of weight, in those made for the American market, would greatly increase the sale of the article.

There is one rule to be observed in loading, for long shots, with *loose* shot—to increase the powder and diminish the shot. The reason for this is obvious : you need increase of power to penetrate, which you *cannot* have, if shot is proportionally increased with the powder. This rule is very often violated. Persons are apt to give too little attention to the *relations* of powder and shot in the charge.

I think that one of the first things a man should do, after (if not before) purchasing a new gun, should be to go out and try it, with all the numbers of shot from eight up to one, to ascertain what numbers it *disperses most evenly*. Supposing your gun to shoot *strong*, the next thing is this evenness of dispersion ; and some guns do best with certain numbers, and some with certain others. Having ascertained which *your* gun affects, use *them* of course. My own opinion is that barrels finely finished *inside* show their superiority most strikingly in throwing the small sizes.

No man who knows anything about shooting, will ever use any other plain wad, than *Baldwin's* patent. Mr. Mullin informs me, that if they are saturated with melted *sheep's fat*, they clean the barrel admirably. I firmly believe this, and I especially believe also in the free use of oil on the inside and outside of a gun. This is considered heterodox by many, but I adhere to what I find to be of practical utility, in my own experience. Another excellent cleaner is *Eley's Patent Concave Felt Wad*. It will also improve the shooting of any gun. Shot disperse more evenly before it than before any thing else. In buying them, it is best to select a number larger than your bore, for then the concavity is less likely to be affected by ramming. The only objection to them is their high price : they retail here in Montgomery at $1 50 a bag. Nevertheless it is cheapest to use them at all such game as turkeys, ducks, &c.

I have gained some practical ideas by looking occa
sionally at the exhibit of the number of pellets to the
ounce, of each variety of shot.

The following tables are taken from Hawker :—

MOULD SHOT				NO. OF PELLETS TO 1oz.
LG				$5\frac{1}{2}$
MG			[hardly]	9
SG				11
SSG				15*
SSSG				17
PATENT DROP SHOT.				
AA				40
A				50
BB				58
B				75
1				82
2				112
3				135
4				177
5				218
6				280
7				341
8				600
9				984
10				1725

Nothing I could add to this chapter would be half so useful as the following extract from " Dinks on Dogs," a most
admirable little work ;

"And now methinks I may safely add a few words on
guns. This, of course, especially to the rising generation.
I need not tell you not to put the shot all in one barrel and
the powder in the other, though I have frequently seen it
done, yea, and done it myself, when in a mooning fit; but
I will say, never carry your gun at full cock, or with the
hammers down, than which last there cannot be anything
more dangerous. The slightest pull upon the cock is

* Best and most perfect of all mould shot.

sufficient to cause it to fall so smartly on the cone or nipple as to explode the cap. Positively, I would not shoot a day, no, nor an hour, with a man who so carried his gun. At half-cock there is no danger. By pulling ever so hard at the trigger, you cannot get it off; and if you raise the cock ever so little, it falls back to half-cock. or, at the worst, catches at full cock. Never over-charge your gun. Two to two and a half drachms of powder,* and one ounce to one and a quarter of shot, is about the load. For summer shooting still less. Never take out a dirty gun, not even if only once fired out of, even if you have to clean it yourself. After cleaning with soap, rubbed on the tow in warm, or better, cold water, without the soap, if not over dirty, remove the tow, put on clean, and pump out remaining dirt in clean warm water, rinsing out the third time in other clean warm water. In-vert the barrels, muzzle downwards, while you refix your dry tow on the rod. Work them out successively with several changes of tow, till they burn again. Drop a few drops of animal oil—refined by putting shot into the bottle , neat's foot oil is best for this—on to the tow, and rub out the inside of barrels with it well. Wipe the outside with oil rag, cleaning around the nipples with a hard brush and a stick; ditto hammers and the steel furniture. Use boiled oil to rub off the stock, but it must be well rubbed in. Before using next day, rub over every part with a clean dry rag. Nothing is more disgusting than an oily gun, and yet nothing is more requisite than to keep it so when out of use. In receipts you will find a composition to prevent water penetrating to the locks, which ought to be as seldom removed as possible. I shall not tell you how to do this, for if you do know the how, where is

---

* I have been long satisfied that this is overcharging, and some of my most successful friends agree with me.

the necessity, and if you don't, in all probability you would break a scear or mainspring in the attempt, as I did, when first I essayed, and after that had to get the gamekeeper to put it together. So your best plan, in this latter case, is to watch the method for a time or two, when you will know as much of the matter as I do. If you want a gun of first rate workmanship, you will have to pay a swinging price. Fifty pounds for a tip-top London gun ; thirty-five pounds for a Westley Richards. One London gun will outwear two of Westley's. Why, I cannot say, but all his barrels are soft. Moore & Gray sent some eighty dollar guns to this country last year, the best and cheapest common guns I have seen. For finish, I would as soon have them as Westley Richards' guns. There is not much choice between any London maker, and there are several Birmingham makers fully equal, if not superior to, Richards. Always keep your powder dry, and in a dry place. Never shoot with anything but English powder, Curtis & Harvey's diamond grain, Hall's glass or rifle, both same quality, and Pigou & Wilks' best powder. There is very little choice between them. They are strong and clean shooting powders. Don't use too large, nor yet too small shot. Six, seven, and eight, are your mark for ordinary work ; for duck, from common gun, number four. Never leave your dog whip at home : you always want it most on those occasions. A gun thirty one inch barrel, fourteen gauge, and eight pounds weight, is as useful an article as you can have. Never poke at a bird, that is, try to see him along the barrels. If you do, you never can be a good or a quick shot Fix your eye or eyes on the bird, lift up your gun and fire the moment it touches your shoulder. Practice this a little, and believe me you will give the pokers the go-by in a short time. It is the only way to be a sharp shot And now I will have done, trusting I have not wasted your time in reading so far to no purpose."

CHAPTER IV.

THE SETTER AND POINTER.

THE dogs in universal use, for the hunting of game birds, are the *Setter* and *Pointer*. The *Cocking Spaniel* or *Springer* (which Forester considers to be the original stock of the Setter), is unknown in the Southern States, and can only be procured with great difficulty at the North. As he will probably not be mentioned again in these pages, it may be as well to remark that he is a very small dog, with some of the characteristic marks of the setter, but having a more *curly* coat and longer ears. He does not set his game, but indicates a near approach to it, by a slight whining. From what I gather about him in the books, I incline to the opinion, that he would be more useful here than in the Northern States. Every sportsman knows how frequently we are balked, by quail betaking themselves to thick black-jack and other coverts. For such ground the *Cocker* is said to be admirably adapted. Birds lie better before him than before the setter or the pointer. I therefore hope that our sportsmen will begin to import them.

The authorities are divided on the question of preference between the setter and the pointer. Each has its good qualities; each its defects. But I have not the slightest doubt, that *for this climate*, the pointer is the proper dog. His tender skin and liability to suffer with cold, are more than counterbalanced by his capacity to endure thirst and heat. In Alabama, at a moderate estimate one-third of the shooting season, from first October to first

March, is made up of days quite too warm for the comfort of the setter. It is often too oppressive to the sportsman himself. The pointer can and does endure it, but the setter takes "fits" occasionally, and frequently compels his owner to cease his amusement, in pity for the sufferings of his dog.

There is another reason why the pointer is better adapted to the South. We have no professional dog-breakers here, and our sportsmen are lamentably *loose* in their ideas and practice of training. The setter *can be* subdued into perfect obedience and the most admirable performance ; but with imperfect training and careless management he becomes utterly worthless, while the pointer is only comparatively so. This is the general rule ; a few setters are as docile, steady and reliable, after having been once well broken, as any pointer.

I will add another objection to the use of the setter here. In a majority of instances, our shooting grounds are infested with that detestable weed which produces what is vulgarly known as the "cuckle-burr." It adheres in large quantities to the long and silky coat of the setter, gets between his legs and chafes off the skin, and makes him both ugly and miserable. It is not long since I saw a specimen of its effects, upon a very fine-looking dog, which had almost lost the power of locomotion by its terrible punishing. The short, satin coat of the pointer offers no hold to the vile thing; and a moment's reflection will convince the sportsman that this immunity is a vast advantage.

I shall conclude this chapter with a letter from Dr. E. B. J., of Macon county, a friend whose opinion on the subject of dogs or their training, I would rather have than any amateur's I know of. "By his works" he may be "known;" his dogs are the best broken in the State.

In chapter six I shall give a letter from Mr. G. W. Cootei,

of New York, a professional trainer of extensive experience, who has kindly furnished me with a description of
his mode, which will be found highly interesting to the
tyro. The subjoined shows Dr. J.'s :

" FRIEND H : Having promised to give you some few
hints relative to the training of setters and pointers, I
proceed to do so with due modesty, feeling my total in-
capacity, as I have had but little experience ; yet, still to
the mere novice, I may give some advice that may enable him, with his own judgment, to train his dogs to his
own advantage. There are several modes of training—
different ways for accomplishing the same end. I simply
propose to suggest the plan that seems most simple to
myself, which I have collected from books, my own *observation*, and the suggestions of others. Some authors will
recommend you to discard the lash altogether ; others to
use it most freely. You may make a good dog with the
lash ; by its indiscriminate use spoil the best. My idea is,
that it is next to impossible to train a dog *properly* without it ; yet it requires the nicest judgment when, and to
what extent, to use it. A dog should never be lashed
until he is made fully to understand the *why*—or, it may
be, in inculcating a lesson that you cannot otherwise en-
force.

" Before giving our few lessons in training, it may not
be amiss to give a few hints as to the selection of a good
pup from the *litter*. I will mention what I consider the
ne plus ultra of a good pup :—well formed limbs, wide
between the eyes—eyes full but not too prominent—
frontal sinuses well developed ; the head broad and full ;
the poll large ; muzzle rather long and only slightly
tapering ; ears rather long, very thin, and angular ; tail
long, small and tapering, presenting a very *rattish* appearance I consider this one of the best marks of good

blood in the English Pointer. The hair short, thin, and
very fine and glossy—this mark I regard above all the
rest, as I think a fine silken coat indicates a nervous,
active temperament—the sense of smell will be apt to be
acute, and I think it almost impossible for him to be
sluggish. In selecting a pup, one should suit his fancy as
to color, as there are good dogs of all colors, but the
lighter for the field the better, for reasons obvious.

"Now for sporting terms. I notice that H., in his
'Chapters on Shooting,' discards from his nomenclature
one term I consider of much importance, i. e. *hie on!*
This is one of the first I teach my young dog. I do not
use it to make him flush, but there are many instances
where it is useful in the field. Our young sportsmen (as
I only write for very young 'uns, being one of 'em myself), will be better able to see its use after reading my
few lessons. I think it all important that sportsmen
should use as few terms as possible; yet I think that another phrase might be introduced into your nomenclature
with benefit—it is *close on.* It is a slang term, not at all
technical, but I use it with great convenience. I perceive that H. is *down* upon all slang terms, and the word
heed ! in particular, and I admit with some justice. Wish-
ing to establish an uniform sporting nomenclature, I can
but admit, I like the word on account of the force and
emphasis with which it may be used. But concurring in
the desire for an uniform sporting nomenclature, like himself, I will discard it, and henceforth use the more techni
cal phrase, *toho !* or *ho !*

"Now for our pupil. We should take him in charge
quite early—as early as the second month—I like to ac-
custom him to obedience from his earliest *puppyhood*, to
engraft upon his very nature *obedience*—and that you cannot do, but by beginning very early. I have *heard* of

dogs running wild until a year old, and then brought into training, but I have never *seen* one *properly* trained at that age. Such an one might satisfy the novice and pot-hunter, that know not what a trained dog is, but the true sportsman would kick such from his kennel. Our pupil's first lesson should be *toho ! steady ! hie on !* and if you admit my slang phrase, *close on*—(pronounced cloze on). These words you can very soon with patience learn him by means of a plate of beef, or such other food as he very much fancies. You should place a small piece of beef in a plate before him. Of course he evinces very great anxiety to 'pitch in.' You repress his ardor, by giving him a slight tap upon the head, crying *toho !* Of course he does not understand the meaning of the word, but every time he starts, check him with a tap, crying *toho !* with emphasis. After repeated trials, he soon associates the word with the slap, and stops of his own accord. After *pointing* for a few seconds, cry *hie on !* at the same time gently forcing him towards the plate. *Hie on !* he learns amazingly soon. A few such lessons and the words are learned, to be retained. The word *steady* is now easily learned, by making him approach the plate slowly, crying *steady ! steady !* at short intervals. When near the plate, cry *toho !* never permitting him to eat until you give the word *hie on !*

"The word *close on* should be used when you wish him to break his point, but not ' *pitch in* ' to the plate ; before he arrives at the plate cry *toho !* and then *hie on !* when he has pointed, by the word *close on*, he must understand that he is to move cautiously, by the oft-repeated command of *steady ! Steady !—close on*, should not be used with the same emphasis as *hie on* and *toho !* With care, these words may be soon learned to the pup—recollecting never to use severity at this age, and that no other hand than your own should furnish him with food, and always bear in mind that you are not to begin a new lesson until the old one is thoroughly understood.

" Your next lesson should be *down charge !* or either of the two words separately—as *down*, or *charge !* This he is made to understand by gently forcing him down, keeping his hind legs well up under him, extending his fore legs, and forcing his head gently between them, crying *charge ! charge !* tapping him every time he moves. Practice him frequently in this position (using only sufficient severity to make him obedient), until he is obedient. Now to make your dog drop at the command, you should cry *charge ! charge !* with your hand upraised ; forcing him *rather roughly* into the required position, and by frequent practice, you will soon have him drop to the word. When you wish him to rise, cry *hie up !* at the same time gently raising him until he understands ; this he will now readily do, as he already associates the word *hie* with action. When your dog behaves well, never fail to encourage him with caresses ; when badly, let him be made to know and feel it. When giving this lesson, you should have your pupil within doors or an enclosure, so that he cannot play the truant. In this instance it may be well to pursue ' Dinks' plan—use a cord, fasten him to a peg ; make him charge ; walk off from him ; if he attempts truancy, the cord retains him ; return, lash him gently, make him charge again ; walk off some distance, still crying charge ! charge ! always with hand upraised. You should practice him until he obeys the summons at any distance. You may now practice your dog every time you feed him, thus : place a portion of his food a few paces from him, make him *charge ! close on ! steady ! steady ! toho ! charge ! close on ! steady ! steady ! to-ho !* (or *ho !) hie on !*

" Now to teach your dog to retrieve. First begin with

something soft—an old glove will best answer your purpose—first make him toy and play with it, then cast it a short distance from you—he will naturally chase it and return with it to you—encourage him with caresses. You should practice this often, always using the term, *hie, fetch!* when you send him after it, and fetch! or *come in!* when you wish him to return. To teach your dog the word *come in,* you should use it upon all occasions when a short distance from you; you may use it when you call him to feed him, &c. To teach him the word, you may let him accompany you in a walk, having a slight cord attached to him. When he plays too far ahead, check him, cry *come in!* if he pays little attention to the summons, draw him in rather roughly by the cord. When you wish to teach him the word *back!* or to *heel* (I prefer the word *back*), you should check him by the word *back! back!* Make him follow behind you, and when he attempts to go ahead give him a tap with the whip (an article the sportsman should never be without). The words are very easily learned. Your pupil should be early accustomed to the call of an ivory whistle, when too far to hear the call *come in!*

" To return to *retrieving.* To teach a dog to *retrieve,* frequently requires a great deal of patience and perseverance; but rest assured when once accomplished, you will be amply repaid for your trouble. You will sometimes hear your friend say, 'my dog will not retrieve; he has no disposition to do so. I cannot make him,' &c. It is not so ! I believe any pointer or setter can be made to retrieve well. After all toying and coaxing fails, then you must try the virtue of the lash, remembering always to use it with moderation, and be very careful that you do not cow your puppy. This is the mode I would recommend. Within your room or yard where you will be undisturbed—recollecting that the presence of company man or dog, should be prohibited. First begin by placing your glove within mouth, make him retain it; if he rejects it, replace it, gently correcting him, crying fetch! fetch! After he understands the meaning of the word fetch, you may let him accompany you in a walk, in some quiet place. Whenever he drops the glove, you must gently and encouragingly replace it, crying, fetch! fetch! If he rejects it, then the lash must be used, though sparingly. If you study the disposition of your dog and manage properly, he will soon perfectly understand you, and gaily and happily gambol along side of you, never daring to drop his charge and if he should, he will only need the words, *hie, fetch! fetch! fetch!* to make him bound back with eagerness after the lost glove. You may now take the glove, cast it from you, and tell him to *hie, fetch!* he will immediately return with the glove. You may now let him see you drop the glove, walk off thirty or forty yards, waive your hand in the direction of the glove, and cry *hie, fetch!* he will of course regain the glove. After practising him at this often, you may drop the glove unobserved by him. He will soon follow your track for a considerable distance for a lost article, by receiving the command, *hie, fetch!* You may now give the glove to another person to hide, first permitting the dog to see it in his possession, and he will be almost certain to find it, if it is at all accessible. In your first lessons be careful that you place the glove where your dog will be certain to find it—not too far off. There is another term or *trick* I teach my dog, that is not absolutely necessary, but it is most easily learned, and I find it quite convenient in the field, and besides it somewhat adds to his accomplishments. It is *hie over*—a command to leap—often necessary to make your dog 'cross fence.' To teach him, you first cry *toho!* to make your dog stand; you then hold tolerably near him a piece of beef,

then use a stick as a barrier between him and it, making it
necessary for him, to leap for it, upon receiving the command *hie over !* If he disregards the word *hie over;* use
hie on ! and afterwards *hie over,* until he understands,
which he soon does by frequent practice. Very soon he
can be made to over leap a chair or cane without the in-
citement of a dainty morsel. A few words of advice, and
your dog is ready for the field. After your dog begins to
retrieve, make him play with the ball—practising all the
lessons with it that he learned with his *beef.* (I usually
begin my first lessons with the aid of beef on account of
the dog's great love for it, and because he is much more
apt to *learn his lessons* for such a prize; but I think it
very improper that he should be fed regularly with it, as
it injures his scent). The ball that I have used and
prefer, is the head of the femur of the ox, nicely covered
with cloth ; the reason why, he is less likely to *mouth* the
birds after using such. He gets into the habit of taking
up his ball easily, as otherwise it would hurt his teeth, it
being of bone. Having made an innovation by the introduction of a slang phrase—i. e., *close on*—I must give my
reasons for so doing. I have frequently been out sporting with dogs not trained to its use, and I have frequently
experienced the greatest inconvenience. If the dog
should have a good nose, and the breeze a little stiff, he
will not unfrequently point a bevy, or even a single bird;
thirty or forty, and even fifty yards. When such is the
case, what is the usual procedure ? Why, you generally
see the sportsman begin to *kick* his dog on, step by step,
thirty or forty yards—a sight not altogether sportsman-
like or gentlemanly, I ween. With a dog taught the
word *close on,* the difficulty is at once overcome. You can
always tell when your dog is very near a bird, so there is
no need of flushing, by the too frequent command of
close on !

"The young sportsman must recollect that he cannot train his dog in a day or a month, but that he must practice him for many montes ; and even so long as the dog should live, he should never be suffered to forget his lessons.

"The above is all that I consider necessary for *house training*. If it should be desirable, I may give a few items to the young sportsman upon his first taking his dog to the field."

CHAPTER V.

FIELD TRAINING.

" FRIEND H : Having promised to give you my mode of *Field Training*,' I propose to give you what I have found to answer best my purpose. Taking it for granted that your puppy Dash has had proper house training, you should select such grounds as will enable you to keep your pupil always in sight. He should be taken out alone at first, unless you find that he is deficient in action. When such is the case, you will do well to take him out with an old, well-trained dog, of fine action ; and it will be well to take them to a field where you will *not* find game. Your object, of course, will be to get your pupil in the way of hunting briskly at a full gallop. He will soon get in the habit of going as you wish. Nothing looks so bad to the eye of a sportsman as a pacing or trotting dog in the field. Most thorough bred dogs will carry themselves handsomely. Taking it for granted that your dog now possesses fine action, you should take him to a field where you will probably find game. In beating the field, always go against the wind; do not let Dash play more than fifty or eighty yards from you, and be careful at first to quarter your ground, to teach your dog to do so—call his attention by a single blast of your whistle—waft your hand to the right diagonally across the field ; when he has gone some eighty yards in the required direction, you will call his attention by another blast— wafting your hand to the left, going yourself in the same direction. By pursuing this course for a short time, you

will soon be enabled to cast him off to the right or left
without trouble. Be careful to call his attention by a single blast on the call—to waft your hand in the required
direction—pursue the same course yourself for a short
time, and it will not be long before you will be pleased
with the result. When you wish him to *come in*, when
at an inconvenient distance to speak to him, repeat the
blast upon the call three or four times. Dash, in his
early days of puppyhood, will be sure to point sparrows
and everything else having feathers that will nestle under
the grass. For this you must not chide him too roughly,
but simply call him off, and pay no attention to the bird;
by no means shoot anything except game before him. By
pursuing this course, Dash will soon heed nothing save
game; but if he shows much perverseness, as some will
at times, the lash must be used. You must expect frequently to have your patience sorely tried with your pupil. You must always keep him in sight, and when he
does strike his first bevy he will be sure to point, if he is
of the right stock, which I take for granted he is, as no
true sportsman will take the trouble of training any other.

" After giving Dash house training and he should refuse
to point his first bird, I would be disposed to turn him
over to the halter. I have a dog which pointed his first
quail when three months old, without ever having seen or
previously scented one; at four or five months of age, he
was as staunch as I could wish—I could control him on
the point, making him charge, close-on, &c. He had
thorough *house training*.

" When you observe Dash more excited than usual, you
may reasonably expect a bevy near. They will not probably be far off, as he has not become accustomed to the
familiar and welcome scent that will enable him to *wind*
them at a distance. Now comes the trying hour for master and pupil The former should be perfectly cool, and

should consider the killing of game a secondary affair—
let him give his attention to Dash. The dog seems too
eager for the scent—you cry steady ! steady !—if he is
apparently near the game, and you are afraid he will flush,
you cry toho ! You approach and find the quail do not
rise—you tell him to close-on, which he does by moving
rather rapidly—you check him by crying steady ! steady !
he points, toho ! You now approach and flush the bevy ;
be sure you bring down one bird, and it will be well that
you only fire one barrel, that you may have more time to
look after Dash, who of course scampers after the whirring
bevy. You immediately cry toho ! come in !—on, on he
goes ; in his wild excitement he disregards your will entirely. You now use your whistle. By this time the
birds are out of sight (but you, of course, have marked
them), and he is running helter skelter. You must soon
get hold of his collar, drag him rather roughly back to
where he *pointed*—lashing him slightly—and make him
charge ! and keep his position until you reload ; after
which you will take him to where your bird has fallen—
indicate the place with your hand, crying *hie fetch ! fetch !
fetch !* From his previous lessons he will know that you
wish him to look for something, and his nose will soon
tell him what it is. Do not let him mouth or toy with it,
or he will soon get in the habit of roughly mouthing your
game, than which I scarcely know a worse habit.

" You may now rest for a short time, that the bevy may
get over their fright ; after which they will be more easily
found, for if they have been very much frightened, they
will not give out sufficient odor to enable your pupil to
point well, and he may consequently flush them, thereby
doing great harm. You cannot do better than to spend
your time in repeating your house training with the dead
quail : casting it from you, telling him to *close-on ! steady !
charge ! hie-on ! fetch!* Cast it some distance unobserved

—waft your hand in the proper direction, and tell him *hie fetch! fetch! fetch!* After a short time has elapsed, you may take Dash to where you have marked the birds. When near the birds, keep Dash near you, that he may be the more easily controlled. If he seem too eager, he only needs the command of *steady!* to control him. Let the command be in rather an undertone—never get into the snobbish habit of *bawling* at your dog. Apart from its being an ungentlemanly habit, it frightens the quail more or less, and they will not lie so well to the dog. Ha! but Dash has *come* down to a point most beautifully, toho! Y u carefully approach, flush and shoot the bird, and immediately give your attention to the dog, crying *charge!* in a strong and emphatic tone; if he breaks, get hold of his collar as soon as possible and lash him, and at the same time drag him to his *point* and make him *charge* and keep his position until you reload. You then cry *hie-up,* make friends with him, and cast him off—he soon points again. You manage to get very near the dog, and when you fire, immediately cry *charge!* and it would be well to accompany " the word with a blow," at this juncture. You make him charge, reload, cry hie-up, indicate the point where the bird has fallen, and command him to hie fetch! He gayly and gladly does your bidding without mouthing your bird. You cast him off again, and *always* manage to control him after you fire—*never, never* suffering him to break shot without feeling the lash. Remember this is the most critical time for yourself and dog. Never suffer yourself to become excited; do not for some time fire more than one barrel, that you may sooner give your attention to Dash, and you will accomplish much if you can be near enough to Dash to give him the lash as he first springs from the point, at the same time crying, *charge!* If you do not suffer yourself to become excited, and lose sight of your dog after your shot, you will soon have him to drop at the report of the gun but rest assured, if you let him have his own way a few times, in your eagerness to secure game, you will rue it for many a day to come. You cannot have this fact too strongly impressed upon yourself. If you control him *from the first*, your object will be attained. If Dash evinces un usual perverseness in this, it will be well to make him *charge* while on a *point*. Even should he see a dead bird fall, he should not retrieve without permission.

" Should you wing a bird, do not suffer him to chase it It is far better that you shoot it again, or that you lose it, than he chase it. You will see the importance of *house training*, and the command *charge* in particular. It matters not at what distance Dash is from you, or how excited he may be, he must be taught to obey the word. More fine dogs have been ruined by suffering them to break shot when young without proper correction, than in any other way. Make this a *point* to be attained, and when secured you have a trained dog, as everything else is early attained. With the exception of making Dash *charge* when there is a bevy whirring about him, he may perform as well as any old and well-broken dog. You can make him *close-on*, *steady*, and *toho*, and keep him upon the point by the command as long as you desire. Never suffer him to flush the game for you, or you may ruin him I came near ruining the best dog I ever owned, by making him flush. He was very young, and under perfect control : I could make him point, close-on, and hie-on to a bevy when I wished. I began by making him flush for me when under thick cover, so that I might have a better snap shot, by being at a proper distance when the bird first rose from the ground. After behaving beautifully for a short time, he concluded that he understood his duty better than I did ; consequently, after pointing as long as *he* thought necessary, he would flush without regard to the command. Sorely, sorely did this mis-step trouble me before I broke him of the habit; but by patience I finally succeeded, by making him *charge* upon the point, and flushing myself."

" When your dog points a hare, be sure to shoot it in its form, and never let him chase it. It is impossible to keep him from sometimes pointing it, but you can and must prevent chasing."

CHAPTER VI.

REMARKS ON TRAINING

THE most that can be done in the way of conveying instruction, in regard to the training of dogs, without practical illustration, is to state the results to be attained, together with an outline of the mode by which to reach them. In practice, the details will necessarily vary very considerably. One man will find this mode, another that, to be most efficient ; besides which, the disposition of the particular animal sought to be controlled, will in a considerable degree affect the character of the training to which he is to be subjected. After all, the knowledge which is to be imparted to sporting dogs, is comprised in the understanding of a very few terms—and the great idea in their education is the enforcement of a *prompt, unhesitating obedience to every command.* For myself, though no great advocate of the whip, I believe that no dog, up to the highest standard of sporting finish, has ever been turned out, without having the great principle of obedience flogged into him, very early in life. A dog may be *coaxed* into performing the *charge*, in a slow, slovenly, reluctant manner ; but whenever you see him drop at the crack of your gun, as if the load were driven through his head, you may set it down that *that* dog associates promptness with escape from severe punishment. I may be wrong ; but my opinion is, that those who would discard the whip entirely, are persons who would not in the field, among dogs which found and pointed birds, know the difference between a perfectly well-broken pointer and a "pot-hunting cur."

In my last chapter I gave the mode adopted by a friend whose success is equal to, if not greater than, that of any Southern sportsman I know. I now present, in his own words, the method of managing dogs practised by Mr. C. W. Cooter, of Havana, New York, a breaker of great experience, and whose establishment, though not large, will be as apt to supply a well-bred and well-broke dog, as any in the country. Mr. C., it will be observed, for convenience, adopts the dialogue form, the purchasing visitor being supposed to be inspecting his kennels :

MR. COOTER'S METHOD.

"C.—As you are desirous to know my method, sir, I will just take this black and tan setter bitch—she is three years old, was brought over the water, and I got her for sixty dollars. Although well broke, she does not come up to some that I have broke in this country, and so I have found all English broke dogs ; the habits of the birds and the covers are so different, that a dog takes two years to become acquainted.

"She was last put to the black and tan dog two years old. You see they resemble each other in shape and style of movement ; these points I consider of great importance."

"H.—Do you not think that the dog would get stronger pups, was he, say, three or four years old ?"

"C.—Unquestionably ; but then as I have none older, I prefer the colors to match, than to put that splendid red dog, although I would do that in preference to any other colors."

"H.—Then you think colors ought to be attended to as well as form ?"

"C.—Certainly I do ; and disposition, constitution and

purity of blood, ought always to be looked at and then we should not have so many indifferent pups in a litter. And I would beg to state here, that I would not cross a setter and pointer upon any account. I have bred many litters, but the trouble comes in when you require to continue breeding. I go for *pure setter* or *pure-pointer*."

" H.—In that, sir, I agree with all my heart."

" C.—When I perceive symptoms of the bitch coming in heat, which she will show five or six days before she will take the dog—I place her and the dog in a safe room together, so as to play—by so doing, I find that the bitch will become more attached, and therefore *mark* her pups more after the dog. As soon as I have seen the bitch stinted, I remove the dog for a day, and then place them together again for another twenty-four hours. I then remove the dog entirely, and as soon as the nine days of heat are *over*, I let the dog and bitch take a walk with me, and if no inclination is shown in the bitch for the dog, I consider her safe to go nine weeks from the first stinting. As I feed all my dogs with boiled Indian meal mixed with cold milk, the bitch gets a share, but if she gets too fat I put her under chain."

" H.—Would you recommend flesh to a bitch ?"

" C.—By no means, as that often breeds mange and humors, which will come out on the pups. I provide a warm bed in a shady situation, and always leave the bitch alone to pup—give her a good clean bed of pine shavings, and remove the dead pups the next day. Let the pups be well fed on new milk and *old* corn mush as soon as they will eat; wean them at five weeks. By applying brine to the slut's teats, you will soon dry her up and have her ready for a hunt. I always let the bitch be loose when suckling her pups."

" H.—Would you use medicine at such times ?"

"C.—If a bitch or dog is sick, I go to the Field Sports of

' Herbert, or ' Youatt,' and take a recipe for the disease, but at all other times I use nothing but stone sulphur in their drinking water."

"H.—Do you keep setter and pointer pups in the same kennel?"

" C.—I prefer not, as I think the pointer requires a warmer house, and so I act, letting the pups out for a run once a week. I couple them two and two together until the open fields are reached, and then turn them loose, and always walk slowly myself in a zigzag way across the field. By so doing they will acquire the habit of quartering their ground. Should any attempt to scale the fence before you, turn your back on him and walk off, giving one sharp whistle—of course you will use the whistle and gun at feeding time every evening."

"H.—But would you not commence breaking the pups in the house ?"

" C.—No, sir ! I have broken many dogs in England, and have handled nearly five hundred in the United States, and my plan has been to let the pups be exercised in the above way, until they are ten months old. I never take a gun in the field, but allow them to hunt and chase without chiding them; by so doing I find they acquire the method of finding birds when they have secreted themselves—it gives them a bolder appearance, and confidence in themselves."

" H.—Why, this is a new idea, and I must know how you proceed."

" C.—As soon as I find that a young dog has got bold in his gallop, and hunts for game—supposing him to be from ten to fourteen months old—I take him with one or two well broke dogs, out very early in the morning, and let *him* run for one or two hours. He will then become a little tired, and in that time will have scared up some game, so that I will know where to take him back to find; but *before I do so,* I couple the pup with *one* old dog ; as soon as the single (broke) dog points, the other broke dog will back him ; or if I hold up my hand, he will stop, which compels the young one to do so ; if not, walk up to the pair, and *push* the pup down ; he will get up, then push him down again, and continue to do so, saying each time *' charge !'* but not aloud, to scare the game—a good box on the ears with the hand will assist this first lesson. Walk backwards each time towards the pointing dog, then *kill the bird ;* the well broke dog will not move whilst you *stand still yourself.* When the gun is re-loaded and capped, say *' hold up !'* or *' whistle ;'* this will start the three in motion ; the old dog will be sure to *point* the *dead bird.* The word *' toho,'* or *' charge,'* will stop the pair, and another box on the ears will get the pup on his belly. Then I pick up the dead bird myself, and walk back to the pup and show it to him—see that he smells the feet, but should he desire to bite it, say *' charge !'* or *' toho !'* and press my foot on his toes ; this tells him he must not catch it. From the time the point was made, you have wasted half an hour. I then follow the same system for an hour or two ; if I do not find game, I discharge the gun at times, and make the dogs ' charge,' and after re-loading, drop my dead bird, *unseen,* and then call the coupled dogs up, showing them as before ; by this time the pup has become docile without the whip. You can then let him loose, but put a bed-cord on him, with a ' rag ' at the other end. He will commence hunting, and should the old dogs make a point, or you think the pup is on the scent of game, walk quietly towards the rag, step on it, and as that stops him, say *' toho !'* Should he be anxious to get on, take the cord in your hand, and jerk him back a foot or two—then say *' steady !'* and as he draws on, stop him again and again, until the bird is *' pointed,'* and then shoot the bird on the ground, if possible. Do not 'yell' or scold, but be as cool as you would in sitting down to dinner among ladies. I have followed this plan for years, *when alone,* and never knew it fail. But let me here state that a man cannot do it who is *desirous to obtain game.* I am well pleased if I can kill from three to five birds in a six hours' tramp. As soon as the young dog begins to lag, kill a few birds over the old ones, and they will be well pleased with their day's work. The next day take your young dog with one old one, put the check cord on the youngster, and see that he does not *commit a fault.* Should he be a wilful dog, you must whip him; but the check cord will do *wonders,* if the master is particular to attend to the young dog. He will now begin to point his game well, and do not by any means allow him to get hold of a bird, but keep him to drop at the discharge of the gun—when told to '*hold up*'—to draw up to the dead bird and *point* it, and then pick it up *yourself.* In three days your pup will be quite a dog. Give him a day's rest at times, but keep at him a part of three or four days a week for six weeks. If the dog is intended for yourself, I would not allow him to 'fetch' the first year; but as I have to break dogs for gentlemen, I have to teach them to 'fetch' before they go home. I therefore adopt the following plan :"

" H.—Do I understand you the pup has not as yet been taught to 'fetch' anything ?"

" C.—Certainly, and for this reason : A dog that has been taught about the house, is often fooled (by a boy) unknown to yourself, and when you desire him to 'fetch,' he will then often cause you a great deal of trouble, and sometimes become hard mouthed ; and again a dog that is taught to 'fetch' will often break '*shot*' when he sees the bird drop."

" My plan is this : After shooting over one or two—I prefer three—young dogs, and they have become per-

fectly steady to *point game,* to '*back*' another dog, to
'drop' at '*shot,*' and to point a dead bird, I take a single
dog into a room, and then show him a live winged bird—
game, of course—after holding the bird and playing with
the dog a few moments, I cast the bird from me, saying at
the same time, '*fetch*' it, in a kind voice. He will most
always do so; if not, play with him again, open the door,
and toss the bird into the darkest corner of the room. He
will then lift the bird, and as he comes out of the door,
catch him, and take the bird away, and reward him with
a piece of cake. I follow this plan two or three times a
day, taking care not to tire the dog of this *new sport.*
Keep him from the field for three days, and then take him
alone, kill game, and see that he *points* his *dead bird* as
before, and then tell him to '*fetch !*' Should a young dog
lift a bird before these lessons, do not chide him, but speak
kind, and walk from him immediately. He will then
come running after you, and then take the bird, but do not
recompense him by flattery.'

"H.—Well, this is a new system, for I have always considered that a dog must be broke under the ' whip.' "

"C.—The whip is a good article in its place, for an old,
headstrong dog, but the *check-cord* is better even than that
in such a case, as it does not cow a dog down like the
whip. I *never walk* up a bird, but, let the dog be ever so
staunch, stoop down and pat him, or even *push* him—for
this reason: how many good shots you will lose if your dog
will not go into a piece of thick brush, and let you stand
on the outside! Should a dog jump on to his game, walk
so as to be able to tread on the check-cord, every foot;
this will make him *creep* like a cat up to his bird. Should
a dog puzzle or nose the ground, stop him at once by the
puzzle peg, which is made in this way: Take a piece of
pine board nine inches long, whittle off six inches to the
size of your finger—the other end should resemble the

palm of your hand. Fix four wire staples at each corner to run a string or small strap to; tie one string at the back of the ears—the other should slip over the tusk of the lower jaw. I once shot with a keeper in Kent, England, who always used it, and his dogs were noted for the style they made their game at a distance."

" H.—Well, sir, I have heard of your dogs being well broken, and I will take a pair. What are your prices?"

" C.—We charge $60 for a pointer or setter that does not fetch, but broken to point live and dead game, and drop at shot, $75, for either pointer or setter that has all the above qualities, and 'fetches.' Should you like your purchase, you or your friends can send us a draft, and state the size they require, also the three best colors they approve of, and we will ship them by express from New York City."

CHAPTER VII.

ADVICE TO THE SPORTSMAN.

AMONG the various contributions I have received from sportsmen in different sections of the country, I find the two which follow. It may be said of them, that each inculcates a good lesson to the gunner. The first illustrates the folly of some good men and good sportsmen in a certain particular; the second, how egregiously the inexperienced hand may be deceived in the character and capacity of a dog. And I will take occasion here to remark, that in my opinion very few dogs are ever too impetuous, or, as it is often termed, *high-strung*, if training is commenced *sufficiently early* and continued assiduously and without interruption. It is, however, a settled thing in my mind, that an animal of the highest degree of courage and game, cannot be allowed to run wild until he is from six months to a year old, and *then* be broken into perfect steadiness with any reasonable amount of drilling and punishment. *Me judice*, the proper age to begin the training of a puppy, is from six weeks to two months. Any puppy of that age can be taught, *in from ten minutes to as many hours*, to obey the order to " *charge*," with perfect promptness. Nothing else need be taught him for some little time ; but a constant practice of *this*, until it becomes a " second nature" to obey it *like a flash*, with his quarters handsomely under him, his paws extended in front, and his head between them *and well down on the ground*—and to remain, with the passiveness of death itself, for half an hour, if required. Day in and day out, should he be practised at this duty, and the more regular and the longer the lessons are, the better dog will he be.

The sketches I subjoin are from a Northern sportsman, to whom I am already under obligations. I give first—

GUNS UP!

OR, A DAY WITH A GOOD SHOT.

Speaking of the improper and careless way in which some sportsmen handle their guns, brings to mind a day's shooting I once had with one of the quickest shots I ever hunted with. We will term him Frank, for convenience. He had written me to inform him when I would have two or three dogs for sale, and the most convenient time for him to come and try them. In answer, I wrote him that I had three, whose colors grouped well together, and which matched well for *size, action,* and *temper ;* and the best time for a trial was about the first of September in the North. He came as appointed, and after a late dinner and segars we retired early to bed. Frank was up early, and dressed for shooting—a clean, laminated steel seven-pound gun, diamond powder, and number seven English shot—a pocket full of caps, and a small flask of brandy. Thus equipped, after breakfast we started for the stubbles close by my house. The dogs had been let loose for an hour, to empty themselves, and now went off with the word *hie-on,* in a dashing style. I will here describe the dogs : " Czar," an orange white setter; "Shot," a red and white, with black tinge on the red, setter; and "Don," a fawn and white pointer. They were all two years old, and the price I put on them was $260. I noticed at start-ing that Frank handled his gun in a careless way, and told him that a gun pointed continually at me was often the cause of making me nervous. His reply was, that I need not fear him, as he had shot for years. As I said

above, the dogs went to work in a gay style, and soon
crossed a couple of fields; when, as we mounted the third
fence, a fine bevy of quail raised and dropped into a cornfield close by, and as the dogs went up the wind, " Czar"
made a *point*, and as I whistled " Shot" and " Don"
turned in their range and backed him ; but as he commenced drawing, the three were soon together—each one
anxious to make the game, but as I had marked the birds,
we went on, and in the next field " Don" and " Czar"
pointed together, ' Shot' backing them a short way off.
We now walked quietly up, and as we came within three
or four yards, the word " *hold-up*," in a gentle voice,
caused them to creep on towards the game ; and now the
three form a picture—each dog points in a different attitude, with tails straight, necks extended, and lips quiver-
ing. I asked Frank if he thought that style suited him.
He exclaimed, " The *sight* is worth a journey to see !"
and at the same time up went the old cock quail. Frank
dropped him in a moment. The dogs dropped at the discharge of the gun, and as I had loaded and capped, a
whistle of gentle tone caused them to raise quietly and
point staunch. A whistle, and they creep like cats for a
few yards, when " burr," " burr," and the whole bevy
flew in a scattered form in all directions. I dropped my
single bird, (shooting as I do with a single-barrel gun).
The dogs "charged." I then turned to Frank, who said
he had got a pair down, and had marked the rest in the
same place as myself. We now re-loaded, and the dogs
being *hied-on*, they went up to the place where the birds
had lain, and then on to the dead birds, which they pointed. I asked Frank to pick up the bird under " Don's"
nose, whilst I picked up the single bird and turned to find
Frank's other brace. The dogs hunted them carefully,
but only found one, and as they seemed to trail towards a
ditch, I got Frank to go and stand above it, whilst I went

with the dogs below to *give* them the *wind*, and as the
dogs hunted carefully, I observed the winged bird dodg-
ing among the weeds; and getting within a couple of
yards, I took the liberty of removing its head. This plan
I prefer, sooner than let the dogs chase after it, as that
often causes dogs to flush the next birds they come to.
While re-loading, I was startled by the shot of Frank's
gun whizzing by me. It appeared, by his account, that
he had placed the gun across his shoulders, and in turning
around, the cock caught by a twig which raised it sufficiently to strike the cap and explode. He had shot a
sapling asunder just about the height of my head, which
caused me to think it a better subject to experiment upon
than the head of a father of six children.

We now went on. Finding three bevies more, Frank
bagged his pair out of each; but as to myself, I was sufficiently engaged in *trying* to dodge the muzzle of Frank's
gun, as he sometimes dropped the same in a line for my
heart, as we mounted a fence, or grasping it with both
hands across his shoulders. He had became so much ac
customed to do so, that his accident nor my continual cau-
tion of " guns up !" had any effect on him ; and he is not
the only good shot that has this bad fault.

We now crossed an old pasture field covered with
whortle berries, and as the dogs neared a corner down by
a swamp they all showed symptoms of game, and as we
came near them, stood in a bold style—when " whirr,
whirr," went a pair of ruffed grouse, and Frank made a
handsome right and left of them. While he was re-loading, three more got up, one after the other, giving me a
good shot. " *Hie-on* " to the dogs, when three more birds
fell to our guns; one being hit in the eye commenced
fluttering, which tempted " Shot" to break from "*charge*,"
and dashing in flushed the rest of the grouse; which
offence was rectified by my dragging him *back* to where

he started from and administering a good strapping, ac-
companied with the words " *charge!* " " *charge!* " After
making friends with the three dogs, by patting them, they
commenced pointing the dead birds. " Czar " had ranged
into the swamp, and on my calling "*fetch,*" he soon returned with a winged grouse.

We now turned towards the places where we had
marked the different bevies—Frank shooting in a most
splendid style. Except the careless manner of pointing
his gun in the direction of your humble servant, and holding his hands over the muzzle when seeing me correcting
the dogs, he was perfection. We now entered the corn
field, and as I cautioned the dogs with the word " *steady,*"
cock after cock got up, but the corn was so high and
the weeds so thick, we could not shoot, or see our dogs ;
and the cocks not being expected there, I proposed to
leave them for after lunch, and then use my pair of
spaniels. Therefore, taking a line for the house, we
crossed the wet grounds that led into the swamp, and
something close to the dogs flapped up and down again
by a bush so quick that I could not tell what it was ; but
the dogs going on soon came to a faint point, and " sceap,"
" sceap," went a pair of jack-snipe,—bang, bang, bang,
and not a bird. I chided the dogs with " *Toho ! toho,
sirs ?*" and then loaded my gun. " Shot " and " Don "
now went off to the left, making a stiff *point,* while
" Czar," on the right, was retrieving a dead snipe, one of
the pair he had marked better than us. We now had a
dozen good shots, bagging nine snipe. We then went to
the house for luncheon and some home brewed ale ; then
taking a segar, we rested ourselves until three o'clock.
I then chained up " Shot " and "Czar." Calling " Don "
to *heel,* we started with " Dash " and " Busy." These
small cockers were handsome—but are *not* the *kind* I
would recommend to the young Southern sportsmen

The dog best adapted for their use is the Sussex spaniel. I have seen them in my native town of Lewes, England, as large as a small setter, with ears from six to eight inches long. Such dogs would be of immense value in cover hunting. Here I would make a mark : As we crossed the field, Frank found a quail in his outside pocket (he had forgotten to search), and placing the butt of his gun on the ground, he held the bird up for me to see, and while he was so doing " Dash" jumped up to get the bird, and as his foot came down, it caught the cock of Frank's gun ; and as the hammer was *down* on the cap *(instead of being at half-cock)*, another explosion occurred,—taking fortunately nothing but Frank's hat brim; but had his *hand* been on the muzzle, one of the best shots in the United States would have been minus a finger or two.

I now sent " Dash " back to the house with the dead Quail. He soon returned, and we then went on towards the cornfield, which was a wet one, and telling Frank to get on a stump in the middle, I *hied-on* the spaniels. As they went barking around, the cock fluttered up and down in all directions, and as Frank shot and loaded as quick as he could, " Dash " retrieved me seventeen good autumn cock, in less than two hours. As Frank had marked a few birds down off by a piece of sprouts, I coupled up "Dash " and " Busy," and then got some nice points with " Don." Bagging a few birds, we crossed a stubble and found a bevy of quail, which finished our day's sport

On counting our game, we figured thirty-seven quail, six ruffed grouse, twenty-one woodcock, and ten snipe, which I think, in the North, a good day for three barrels and no marker. Frank, in his letters, when speaking of his " Don," " Czar," and " Shot," concludes with ' Guns Up !' "

The reader will not fail to note in the following how terribly severe was the training required to subdue a high-spirited dog—unsubdued by previous *early* discipline and steady work :

DOG DEALING, OR TAKING A LESSON.

Some twenty years ago I was presented with a splendid silver-and-white Pointer, of noted stock, in the south of England. Being young myself and my old dogs nearly worn out, I named him " Ponto," and if a dog was ever worshipped, I believe " Ponto" was my idol, and at three months old he would "*fetch* " and " *charge.*" I believe he was as well house-broke as a dog could be up to six months of age, when I thought I would commence shooting over him. I must here state that the stock of " Ponto " was once so fine that a fox hound was introduced, which gave the breed plenty of foot, and of that " Ponto " was a miracle. Well, I hunted " Ponto " nearly three months, and could do nothing with him when he came on game ; although he would point a winged bird in the house, &c. One day a friend who shot on an adjoining estate, came to a spring where I was drinking, and offered me a very nice pair of broke dogs for " Ponto." I told him I could do nothing with him except *show him in the house or yard.* His answer was, that if *he* could break him, he would suit him, instead of paying a duty on two. I traded, and had by far the best of it, as I thought ; but judge of my surprise, when I received an invitation to shoot with my neighbor two weeks afterwards over " Ponto." I went with reluctance, as I expected to be annoyed as of old, and even took my pair of dogs along. But Bill said " Ponto " would do all the work we would want, and so it proved—notwithstanding the wind (it being in November). We shot over " Ponto" six hours,--killing pheasant, partridge, and hares over

points,—Bill not speaking a harsh word to the dog all
day. The dog retrieved, after pointing dead in every instance ; and before the day was out, I offered ten guineas
and the pair of dogs back, but I never was the owner of
" Ponto " again. After dinner Bill gave me his method
of fixing " Ponto," by stating that he got the dog fond
of him, and on the fourth day put a large bag of shot
round " Ponto's" neck, and then mounting his horse rode
the distance of forty miles—the dog ranging where he
chose. The next day the same dose ; and as soon as he
got home, took some dinner, and put a long cord on-
" Ponto," the shot remaining around him besides. At
three o'clock " Ponto " was going over a stubble flushing
the remnant of three coveys of Partridge. Bill then took
him to where he had marked the birds, and by continually
placing his foot on the cord compelled him to stop without speaking to him. He continued this until the dusk
of evening, when he and "Ponto " went home well-
pleased with each other, and both tired out. Early next
morning Bill took his gun and commenced hunting in
earnest, with " Ponto " fixed as before, and, after paying
particular attention to "Ponto," succeeded in killing six
partridges over points. He now hunted him four days
longer with the cord, and then hunted him loose as I had
done, and the result can be seen from my day's hunt with
him. Bill was offered long sums for " Ponto," but said
as he could do a week's work as well as a brace, he was
what he wanted. Since then I have handled nearly five
hundred dogs, and have never seen " Ponto's " equal. I
am satisfied that it was my fault and not " Ponto's," as I
commenced letting him "*fetch* " in the field, before I
taught him in the field to "*point*" game, and I never gave
him—he being so high-strung—sufficient work, and was
too anxious to bag game.

CHAPTER VIII.

ON THE SHOOTING OF QUAIL.

BEFORE introducing a portion of a chapter of *Forester's Field Sports*, I propose to offer some remarks of my own, in regard to the shooting of *quail*. Hereafter I shall give the experience of a friend of mine who has given a laudable attention to the habits of the bird and the mode of hunting him.

Perhaps I shall have no better opportunity than just in this connection, to express the contempt with which every well-bred man must view the practice of taking quail in *nets*. It is a practice which obtains quite extensively in this region, and which will continue while gentlemen sportsmen treat those who are guilty of it as anything else than pot-hunting vagabonds. I do not mean that all who indulge in the villainous practice are worthless characters— though a majority of them are—but that the thing itself is so vile an outrage upon all sportsmanship, humanity, and magnanimity, that no man who *knows better* ought to countenance his best neighbor if he will not discontinue it. We have now in Eastern Alabama a great abundance of quail, except in certain *netting* localities. Where they are taken in that way, the bird is absolutely swept away, in particular neighborhoods. I have known a thousand birds captured within a week, by two or three parties using these infernal machines during a cold, sleety spell of weather when the quail is always loth to take wing.

Another mode by which the quail is decimated, at least

is by traps. These are set mostly by boys and negroes, in plantation enclosures. Two or three active sportsmen, however, will generally keep trapping down, by kicking the little pens to pieces wherever they find them; and they are almost certain to come upon every one within the range of their shooting. Those who take an interest in the preservation of *game birds*, ought by all means to prevent their servants from trapping the bevies which feed on their plantations.

There are a good many yet who are disbelievers as to the faculty of withholding its scent, which most sportsmen attribute to the quail. The fact is of such frequent occurrence, that I should despair of making a fair sportsman of any one who had never noted it for himself. A majority of bevies will resort to this means of self-preservation the second time they have been badly worried by the sportsman. I have observed that the full bevy attacked for the first time rarely does so.

When it is discovered that birds are withholding the scent—that is, when, after having accurately marked them, your dog fails to point upon coming where you *know* they settled—the best plan is to go off and sit down for half an hour. Rest your dog and yourself. By the time you have accomplished this, if you will return to where the birds settled, depend upon it, your dog will begin to *come down* handsomely. I have tried this time and again, and I do not remember that it ever failed.

In regard to *running bevies*, there is one point as to which I differ with *Forester*. He recommends, when the bird is disposed to act thus, an attempt, by taking a circuit, to come around on the opposite side, which is likely to make the birds stop and huddle. This it undoubtedly generally does do; but in this country, if you attempt to cut off the bevy from its covert in the branch swamp or the blackberry briar patch, it will lie until you kick it up

almost, and then whizz under your very nose in the original direction. I know no more awkward shots than those
thus obtained. I prefer following the birds, with the precautions mentioned by Forester, (checking the dog with
steady! steady! toho!) When they reach the grass at
the edge of the swamp, or the old fence near by, ten to one
they will lie. You put them up, and take the chances for
snap shots as they pitch into the covert. I have had a
pretty good experience in heading off bevies, and my deliberate opinion is that it will not pay.

The morning—early morning—is much the best time
for shooting quail. The heavier the dew, or frost, the
better. It has two advantages : the birds lie better, and
the scent is much stronger.

The dry sedge fields (that is, fields turned out to rest,
and grown up with tall sedge grass,) afford the finest
sport. The birds, however, seldom frequent these to any
great extent until the peas of the cornfield are exhausted.
While these remain, the quail lies close by in his covert,
and a very short time, morning and evening, suffices to
fill his craw with his favorite grain. However, if you can
find sedge surrounding a stubble field, lately in oats or
wheat, you may expect great sport early in the season.

In shooting quail, most persons fire too soon, and in
their ardor fail to hit. The truth is, if two birds are
simultaneously flushed and fly off in different directions,
there is just about time enough for a fair shot, of good
nerves, to kill both, cleverly within range. Your first
bird may be taken down at twenty to twenty-five yards ;
your second, at thirty to forty-five. But the tyro *will*
bang away as soon as the birds get up ; and it takes some
time to show the green hand the absurdity of shooting
without aim, through the just risen bevy, expecting to
kill a dozen, more or less. It is seldom that more than
one is thus got, and it is generally mangled, because the

shot have not had time and distance enough to disperse properly. I was always the awkwardest of hands to shoot at bevies, and, finding this to be the case, for convenience sake endeavor always to take down the extreme bird on the right and on the left. This prevents, to some extent, the confusion that besets me inveterately when I keep my eyes on the centre of the whirring crowd.

Marking birds accurately is very difficult. It can only be acquired by experience. Green hands are invariably deceived. *Forester* gives as a rule (and it is a good one), never to believe a bird settled no matter how low he may have been scudding, at a particular point, unless *you have seen a flap of his wings.* He is down then, *sure!*

I give now an extract from *Forester :*

" I have found it impossible to get up early enough to do execution from any country tavern, if one waits until a hot breakfast is prepared. My method, therefore, is to take with me a cold ham, or a cold hunter's round, and to have the table laid over night, in addition to that, with bread, butter, and cold milk, on which, for my part, I can breakfast very satisfactorily.

" This done, if you know the country, go to the place where are the most and likeliest grain stubbles lying near to good woodland or coppice covert, and beat them regularly, in such a manner that the woods shall be down-wind of your beat. Let your dogs, however, beat every field up-wind, by which means they will scent their birds one-third farther than if you go down-wind.

" Look especially to the sides of the field, particularly if they are bushy ; quail do not affect the middle even of the stubbles on which they feed.

" If your dogs trail a running bevy, never run or hurry them. They are, if you do so, nearly sure to flush them wild. Be, on the contrary, very steady yourself, and cry " Steady! steady! toho!" words to which dogs should

be accustomed early. If they point firmly, and are so
very staunch that you can depend on them, it is not a
bad plan to make a wide circuit, and get ahead of the
bevy, which even if wild and running, will often squat on
finding itself enclosed between the dog and the gun, and
thus afford good shooting.

" If you drive a bevy of Quail into good covert, be not
in haste to follow it. It will stay there, be sure; and you
will find them far more certainly after half an hour has
elapsed. For myself, I have found it the best plan,
where woods are small, and the covert thick, to go on
beating the open fields, without following the bevies at
all, in the first instance, marking them down carefully
when they rise, until the feeding and running hour has
passed,—then to follow bevy after bevy, whither you have
seen them alight; and knowing their whereabout, if not
the exact spot where they lie, the dogs will soon find
them.

" Otherwise, if one wastes the morning in killing off one
bevy, by the time he has done with it, the birds will have
crept away into their hiding-places, and he may hunt the
wood-skirts and brush-holes all day along, without finding
another, even where they abound, unless he blunder upon
one by chance.

" During the heat of the day, if one have not found
birds in the morning, although it is pretty much chance
work, bog meadows, brown bushes on southerly and
westerly hill-sides, old pastures with much bent and rag-
wort, and the skirts of coppices, are generally the best
ground, though in some regions they will be found in
large open woodlands.

" In the afternoon, soon after four o'clock, the bevies
again begin to run and feed, and in this part of the day
they will frequently be met running along the grassy
margins of streams which flow through pasture-fields,

whither they resort to drink, or at least to crop the wet herbage.

" So good is the chance of sport at this time, that I would urge it strongly on the sportsman who has failed of finding his bevies on the feeding ground in the morn ing—if he *know* that there is a fair show of birds in the district—not to persist in wearing out himself and his dogs, by fruitless toil in the heat of noon, but rather to await the cool afternoon, when he will very often make up for lost time, and make a heavy bag when circumstances looked least auspiciously.

" I have now set my sportsman fairly in the field, and shown him how best he may find his birds,—more is beyond my means.

"A crack shot must in some sort be born ; but most persons with good eyesight, and steady nerves, may attain to respectability, if not excellence, in this gentlemanlike and manly art.

" To this end, practice and coolness are the great desiderata. Rules, I think, avail little, if anything. I have seen men shoot excellently who closed one eye to take aim—excellently who shot with both open,—never, however, I must admit, decently, who *shut* both—not, by the way, a very uncommon occurrence with beginners. I have seen men again shoot excellently, carrying their guns at full cock—excellently, who never cocked either barrel till in the act of firing.

" There is, however, one thing to be observed,—no man can shoot well in covert, or at snap shots, who follows his bird with his gun, or dwells on his aim—the first sight is always the best ; and it is *deliberate promptitude* in catching this first sight which alone constitutes—what my poor friend, J. Cypress, Junior, used to call the rarest work of nature—a truly cool, truly quick, *crack shot*."

CHAPTER IX.

DUCK SHOOTING—THE MALLARD.

Of all the shooting that I know anything of, in this section, duck shooting, in favorable localities, affords by all odds the finest sport. The mallard, especially, is a game bird of the first order. He is strong and swift of pinion, and, when once alarmed, difficult of approach. Few birds carry off shot better than he; and the gun and the gunner that take him down, regularly and certainly whenever he gets up, within range, need both to be a little better than "middling." At the first of the season, perhaps, this duck will show himself quite unwary, and may be killed with ease in any of the ponds he frequents. But shoot about his resort a few times, and you will then have to deal with one of the most watchful and cunning rascals in the world. It will not happen once in an hundred times that you will see him as soon as he sees you His keen vision descries you two or three hundred yards up the creek, as you crawl stealthily along, and if ever once before frightened by man, he will take wing on the instant. His sense of hearing is most wonderfully acute : break but a twig, however small, and at once he is upon his guard !

The mallard is common to all waters of the South. After the "first cold spell in November," our rivers and many of our creeks contain hundreds of the species. With them we most commonly find the beautiful wood duck, commonly known as the *striped head*. In the waters of the *Alabama*, very early or very late in the season, a great many *green or blue-winged teal* accompany the mallard in his visits ; the former appearing in the fall, the latter in the spring.

Most of our shooting in the interior is done on the numerous creeks into which the ducks go in large numbers from the rivers. Very cold weather, when high winds prevail, is sure to drive up thousands of them to the better-protected waters of the smaller streams. At first, as I have hinted above, they are apt to be anything but wild ; first-rate opportunities are plentiful to get shots at large flocks—but presently they change their tactics entirely, and if they continue numerous, must be approached in the most artistic manner to get shots at all. As a general rule, however, on the streams they frequent they usually have favorite spots for feeding or disporting themselves, to which they quite regularly resort. It is important, then, to the hunter, to acquaint himself with these localities, and to *mark their approaches accurately.* For instance, here is quite a deep hole of eddy water just at this bend of the creek. At its lower end, a log crosses the stream, and on it the ducks frequently may be seen standing in a long row. There is but one—just one—way in which the hunter can escape their observant eyes. Before he has got within two hundred yards of his game, (as he goes down the creek,) he must take a circuit out from the stream—out far enough to prevent the possibility of his being seen. When arrived at a point exactly opposite the eddy water, he takes a " bee line" for it—taking care only to avoid noise ; for the high bank on the side of the creek he is on, shuts him out from the view of the ducks completely. He is thus able, by careful threading of his way, to creep up on the unsuspecting flock, and put one barrel in on the water, and the other as they rise. Had he omitted the *detour*, he would almost inevitably have been brought by the winding of the creek into some posi-

tion whence he could be seen by the ducks, and would
have obtained no shot. It is of the first consequence,
then, in duck-shooting on creeks, *to know your ground accurately*. If you have a companion, too, who is also well
informed as to the haunts of the birds, it is all the better.
It is usual with ducks, disturbed on streams such as we
indicate, to fly only one, two, or three hundred yards,
from one favorite spot to another. This enables two persons to hunt them to great advantage. Thus A and B
are points on the stream at which the ducks feed. You
and your friend are hunting down the creek. You, before getting within ear-shot of A, make such a *detour* as
I have described above, and by means of it *approach* B,
within clear shot of which you lie *perdu*, awaiting the
operations of your friend at A, which is, say, a couple of
hundred yards above you. He steals upon the ducks at
A, fires upon and rousts them, and they incontinently
direct their flight down to B, where you await them. In
the act of settling on the water, you give them one barrel, and as they rise in thick confusion, with a terrible
flapping and quacking, you put in your second barrel
with terrible effect. Your friend then slips around to
the distant point D, and conceals himself, while you
roust them from the intermediate point C, and drive
them down to him. In this way two men will generally
kill a great many ducks, if they are patient, light of foot,
and know the ground accurately The last is the main point.

Shooting on the rivers is generally done by two parties,
in as many canoes; whereof one keeps under the willows
of one bank, and the other of the other bank. It is usual, I believe, to have two gunners—one in the bow and
the other in the middle of the boat—and a paddle in each
boat. Each canoe hugging the shore, (near which the
ducks are generally found,) and proceeding *pari passu*
the ducks often afford shots to both parties.

Generally in these hunts, tents, etc., are taken along, and the hunters, going slowly and carefully along through the day, make it convenient to get out with their luggage, late in the afternoon, near some *roosting ponds.* Some of the party arrange the camp on the river bank, while others go to the ponds to shoot the ducks as they come into roost. There is no finer sport than this. However, like most good things, it does not last very long. The ducks come in between sundown and dark, and the more they have been shot at, the later they make it in going to roost. Other things being equal, it is much better for the sportsman to stand so as to face the west. The lingering rays, (the ducks being between him and the departed sun,) assist a great deal. If it is a good pond, and the hunter is full early at it, most probably as he is going off into a fit of abstraction, he is roused by a distant plaintive whistle—the note of the wood duck—and the next thing is a sharp whizzing overhead, and then a sudden plump of perhaps a dozen *striped heads* into the dark placid waters before him. Presently a far-off *quack* is heard, and in a moment a flock of mallard whizz by him. Crack! crack! at this end of the willowy pond; and as they rush on with cleaving wing, crack! crack! at the other end. These are the advance parties. Directly they come in thick and fast. Wood duck on this hand, mallard on that! Whistle and quack are heard on all sides; from all quarters they burst in—the air is thick with them, and the water in a continual splash. But it is growing darker every minute. There, opposite you, is an open space between the thick branches of the swamp trees. Keep your gaze on *that*—every now and then it is darkened with the rushing crowd. Pitch it into them, coolly. Load and reload calmly but quickly; and when it is too dark at length to shoot, why, perforce, you must desist. Your dog, if you have one, must be kept at work retrieving

It is of no use to go to one of the ponds "in the morning" to recover your ducks. The minks will have left you nothing but a few feathers.

Immense numbers are killed in this way, by experienced hunters. Like every other thing, however, simple as it seems, a little experience is necessary to give one "the hang." The excitement to a beginner is very apt to be overwhelming. The ducks come in with a flight so rapid —from this side and that—the ring of their pinions and their cries make so mingled a din—their numbers are often so great—that the tyro cannot but be confused. This will soon wear off, though, and then the man who loveth our art is "in clover." With his rough retriever—half bull terrier and half setter, or perhaps with the blood of these and a dash of Newfoundland to give him more weight bone and endurance—he knows that so soon as the shooting is over, he can recover all his game from among the willows and flags of the pond. So he blazes away while Don remains quiet, half hid by an old log, with only his head half raised, and his eyes gleaming, as he recognises the sound of the wings of the approaching squadrons. He knows full well that *his time* will come directly.

CHAPTER X.

A WOODCOCK STORY—QUAIL.

IT is rare in this region that we have a chance at Snipe and Woodcock; notwithstanding, season before last, myself and sporting friends managed to kill eighteen or twenty Woodcock (speaking of Woodcock, thereby hangs a tale), and quite a number of Snipe. Notwithstanding Snipe will sometimes afford fine sport, even in this region, I would advise you by all means to keep your pupil from their *baleful influence.* I never knew a young Pointer to hunt them without its doing him great harm. They will rarely lie well to the dog, consequently he soon becomes unsteady. None save an old and staunch dog should go after Snipe. Such has been my experience, as well as that of my sporting friends.

Speaking of Woodcock above, I mentioned that thereby hangs a tale. I must give it to you : You must know I have a female friend who is decidedly *fast* for her age. She is perfectly *au fait* upon anything appertaining to literature, music, science, and the *table.* She is decidedly epicurean in her tastes, and while suffering from the demon Dyspepsia, often has been the time I have been benefited by her *nice things,* &c. (God bless her ! may her shadow never grow less !) You must know that a few months agone she paid a visit to the city of Gotham, where her epicurean taste was delighted with the game of the season, Woodcock among the rest. Frequent, earnest, and spicy were her dissertations upon the game birds of the North—Woodcock in particular. Well,

while out one evening with dog and gun, an unlucky
bird, with a large black body and *very red* head chanced
to pass within range of my gun. I fired, and redhead,
vulgarly called Woodcock, was brought down. I proposed to my sporting friend that we should try and pass
it upon Miss —— as the Simon-pure game bird. He
acceding, when we returned, I hastened with a gleeful
countenance to lay my prize before my fair friend, telling
her that I had just killed a great favorite of hers—a
Woodcock—and that she should prepare it for herself
alone. She hearing its name—Woodcock !—(Oh, ye !)
was perfectly delighted. Some one near, not so epicurean
in taste, cried out, " Miss ——, you are not going to eat
that are you ?" " Isn't it Woodcock ?" " Yes—but I
wouldn't eat *that thing*." " Oh, you don't know what is
good ; it is a regular *game bird*—highly prized in New
York."

Well, the upshot of the matter is this : the joke was
carried farther than I intended. I purposed to have it nicely
cooked, as only she could have it done, and have it brought
upon the table, and then I would make an exposure. But
it so happened that I was compelled to go into the country that night, and did not get back until 10 o'clock next
day. I had forgotten all about the joke, but when I
saw Miss ——'s countenance it recalled the idea I had
of Tam O'Shanter's wife when she was "nursing her
wrath to keep it warm." And didn't I catch it, hot and
cold ? " To treat me *so bad*," " I couldn't believe it of
you." I asked an explanation——" That Woodcock ! too
bad, ugh !—oop-oo-oop, arr-e !—too bad." And when she
looked up so thought I. The cream of the joke I missed
by being absent from breakfast. She, with a sparing
hand, proffered to help those at table. Only one would
partake, and she couldn't *swallow* it. The epicurean lady
ate it with a decided *gusto ;*—rich, rare and spicy were

her plaudits of the game bird, the peculiar *game* flavor, &c. But enough ; the joke was really carried farther than I intended, and I am sorry for it, as my fair friend cannot bear a game bird to this day.

Friend H., you requested me to give you my views in relation to the power of Quail to withhold scent. With myself for a long time it has been a fixed fact, as also with most of our amateur sportsmen. I see the fact mentioned by Herbert, Skinner, Lewis, *et al*. Each one speaks of it as being a voluntary act of the bird; and if not voluntary, that they are aware of their possessing the power. I believe neither: I look upon the fact not as *instinct*, nor anything out of the common laws of nature. I account for it altogether by supposing that excessive terror has checked the usual secretions or effluvia that, in a state of quietude, is given out by the bird, by which the dog is enabled to scent them. If you look in *Carpenter's Human Physiology*, you will find that sudden and excessive terror will immediately check the lacteal secretion, and this is not the only secretion that is checked by fright. Every one has heard of fright producing gray hairs. They say that they are conscious of the power or property, or they would not lie so close—allowing you almost to set foot upon them before moving. I think it is owing to their excessive fright. Terror in the first place checks their secretions, and in the next prevents flight, as they feel as secure in one place as another. See how readily fright will confound the fawn, the hare, and other timid animals, and some birds. I have even heard of birds being checked in their flight by the yelling of a large number of persons, underneath them ;—the birds would drop almost as if shot. Every schoolboy is familiar with the practice of surrounding the hare and then setting up an unearthly yelling ;—the hare in most instances will become so confounded that it may be picked up by hand

It is the same fright that keeps the Quail under cover, although hunter and dog may be very near.

It may be possessed not only by one bird, but a whole bevy may possess the power or property. I will mention an instance : I had spotted several bevies near our village. With one I always had great difficulty—scarcely ever obtaining more than one or two shots. When I would flush the bevy, the birds would rise wildly and fly to all points of the compass. Their motto seemed to be, "Every one for himself, and the devil take the hindmost." I have never before or since seen so wild a bevy. Even when I had closely marked a single bird, I rarely obtained a shot. At the time to which I allude, my dog pointed them at their usual haunt, and to my utter surprise they rose well together, and settled in a beautiful cover for sport, at a short distance. My friend and myself marked them well and closely. Not knowing the Quail as I now do, we immediately pushed after them, anticipating fine sport. We beat the ground again and again—circled the spot to see if they had left—we made our dog hunt very closely, but not a feather could we raise. My dog did not evince by his action that a single bird was near. We beat around the spot at least half an hour, wondering what could the matter be, and rather disposed to blame the dog. (And by-the-by, friend H., let me whisper this fact— there is not a better nose in Alabama, for Quail, than Roscoe's.) Thinking that we or the dog (one) must be misled, we were about giving them up, when one rose directly under me, and then whirr, whirr, they went all around us —the dog in the very midst, and *he* did not point ! How can it be accounted for, unless the secretions were checked by fright ? To prove my views I will mention another case, wherein the same effect was produced by a fright from the hawk. Some sporting friends of mine were approaching a field when they saw a hawk soaring with a

Quail in its talons. They leisurely pursued their way through the field, where they were induced to rest a few moments—the dogs at the time at their heels. After resting for a short time, they were startled by the uprising of a bevy all around them and in their very midst. Now the effect of withholding scent was undoubtedly produced by the depredation of the hawk; it was of course not produced by the sportsmen and dogs, as they had not been flushed. If it was a voluntary act on their part it was altogether superfluous to hold it from the hawk, who obtains his prey alone by sight. When physiology tells us that fear will in many instances, even with *human* beings, check secretions, it is not difficult on my part to believe the same cause will produce similar effects upon the Quail.

CHAPTER XI.

PARTRIDGE SHOOTING.

I AM greatly indebted to my friend, Samuel Swan, editor of the *Southern Military Gazette,* for the use of the following spirited sporting articles, from the pen of the accomplished and versatile author of *"Field Sports."* Mr. Herbert's descriptions have never been excelled; no living literary artist equals him, in my opinion, in that sort of limning which is accomplished by a few dashing strokes. In " My First Day's Partridge Shooting," and " The Yorkshire Moors," he is fully himself. They were never in print before, having been written for Mr. Swan's Gazette, just as that periodical was discontinued by its proprietor in consequence of the large increase of his business, leaving him no leisure to attend to it. I present first:

MY FIRST DAY'S PARTRIDGE SHOOTING.

At last I was eighteen years old. I had been in the sixth form at Eton more than six months; had been promoted from round jackets to long-tailed blue coats, the height and front of the Etonian's ambition; from a pony to a fifteen-hand thoroughbred hack—which I believed to be the best hunter in the island—and from my seat at my sister's governess's table to a knife and fork in the dining room; and now I was to be promoted from shooting rabbits, snipe, wild fowl, larks, and such other animals of the half-game order, to the dignity of a game certificate and a license to kill game in my own right throughout England.

I was already more than a fair shot, for it had been agreed between myself and the governor that I should be entitled to claim a game certificate so soon as I could kill nine out of the first twelve skylarks that should get up before me—the sky-lark when he does not rise to sing flying low, very swiftly, close to the ground, by no means unlike a snipe, and quite as difficult to kill.

This feat I had accomplished some three weeks before the first; my certificate was bought; my first shooting jacket built; my gun cleaned for the tenth time within the last two days; my shot-pouch and powder horn filled; and I, filled full from head to foot with anticipation of distinguishing myself before the eyes of the governor, went to bed, but not to sleep, on the night of the thirty-first of August.

I was awake and on foot at day-break, and it seemed hours, nay years to me, before my father made his appearance, rigged for the field, at about eight o'clock.

Well, to the field we went, in the home farm, and within five hundred yards of the house; in a fine turnip field, knee deep among the broad green leaves, the dogs came to a point. I had made some trivial wager with the governor that I would bag my first bird, a dog-whip or whistle, or some such trifle; but my heart was as much set to win as if a million had been at stake.

Three young birds rose, two crossed the governor to the right, and both fell to his two barrels killed clean. My bird fell, likewise, but he was wing-tipped only, ran and was not retrieved.

I had lost my wager, and my heart was heavy—the governor chaffed me and laughed at me—I grew nervous—got out of sorts—blazed right and left at everything. I carried both barrels at full cock then; everybody did so in those days—missing it before it got five yards away—was quizzed and laughed at more and more, and came

within an ace of being destroyed and rendered worthless
as a shot forever.

Suddenly, in a desperate situation, I took a desperate
resolve : I would never again, while I lived, cock a gun
till the bird was on the wing at which I was about to fire.
No sooner said than done. I let my gun down to the half
cock and proceeded. The next ten birds that rose I put
up my gun to my shoulder without cocking it—pulled—
no fire came, and I got quizzed more and more, and, at
last, actually scolded, as if I were holding back my fire
purposely, because I could not get what I considered a
true aim.

Then I was lectured on the beauties of a *first sight*,
and on the inutility of picking after my birds and on the
danger of becoming a pottering shot ; all of which I knew,
every iota, as well as my monitor. But not a word deigned
I in reply, either in defence or in explanation.

At last I got the hang of it. I cocked my gun as I
raised it, discharged it as the butt struck my shoulder, and
of course killed my bird. I killed thirteen birds, one
after the other, in unbroken succession, four of them double
shots. Then I missed one bird, killing its mate with my
second barrel, and five more in succession ; then two
misses and eight kills, each after each.

At nightfall I had bagged twenty-seven birds out of
twenty-nine shots, after missing some nineteen or twenty
shots without a single kill in the morning. I have never
done much better since. That morning made me all that
I claim to be at this moment, a *deliberately* prompt shot.
But you had better believe, gentle reader, that from that
day forth, to this, I have never cocked my gun till I have
seen my game fairly on wing or afoot ; and yet more, till
I have let it go, as far as I intend that it shall go at all;
and I find that I can kill as many snap shots as most
men. Let those who will, carry their guns cocked. I

say *let them*—so that they don't carry their hammers
down on the nipples—it is all one to me. If they do so,
they don't shoot in my company *nohow*; but for my own
use, give me the gun at half-cock and *deliberate promptitude !*

THE YORKSHIRE MOORS.

It is now well nigh thirty years since my first day on
the Yorkshire moorlands. I was then some eighteen years
of age, and in the sixth form at Eton. In the preceding
autumn I had been promoted for the first time to a game
certificate, and had waged war on the gray partridge,
perdia ɔinerea, with such success as to kill my fifteen
brace in one day's shooting, and to gain the repute of being a most promising young shot ; for be it known I had
practised first on hedge-sparrows, field-fares, skylarks
and swallows, and afterward on English snipe, water fowl
and moor hen, which are not included in the category of
game or prohibited to the landless and unlicensed gunner,
until I had acquired the trick of bringing my stock to my
shoulder, my barrel on a level to the eye, and drawing
my trigger-finger with a single motion, and that without
either winking at the flash or shrinking from the recoil.
In short, I was in a fair way to be as good as I was a
keen shot, when few Eaton boys had a soul above a crick-
et-ball or a boat race.

But the moors ! the moors ! the glorious twelfth of
August ! *Hoc erat in votis !* This it was which was to
constitute me a *bona fide* sportsman ; to make me the
pride and envy of my classmates—my classmates ! nay,
but of the country gentlemen, the crack shots, the brag
artists of the south country preserves, to whom a well-
stocked turnip-field or well-filled pheasant covert, was the
noblest scene of their exploits with the gun.

How eager were my days, how sleepless my nights.

as that day of days approached, which was in my
own esteem to raise me to the level of a Cæsar! and
when the missive was despatched to ask permission of the
eccentric but kind-hearted mistress of Fontague's abbaye
and unnumbered acres of "heath and whin and bare wild
moor," how did my heart leap to the sound of the post-
man's horn! how did I strive to anticipate the future, and
when the reply arrived in the affirmative, where was
there to be found one so happy as I? My gun cleaned
and re-cleaned, locks taken apart and put together again,
oiled and wiped dry and oiled again, till every one in the
house was, or at least had good cause to be, utterly
a-weary.

And then my rig for the twelfth—methinks I can see
it as it lay before me now, just from the hands of the
most approved artist in St. James street—point device
according to Gunter. The russet-purple shooting jacket
of light velveteen, precisely the shade of the blooming
heather; the dun-colored tweed waistcoat and trousers,
undistinguishable from the tints of the faded grass and
ling; the stout yet light and easy shoes; the leather an-
kle-gaiters; the purple-cloth shooting cap, with a tuft of
heather and withered fern in the band—all fashioned alike
to excite the jealousy of the rival sportsman and to defy
the most fastidious eye, while it should at the same time
pass before the eyes of the vigilant and fearful moorcock
without awakening his observation—that all spectators
should exclaim, "Capital get up indeed!" "Devilish well
made, and in good taste too! not a bit overdone, like Aston's
liveries there! no one can say that for them!"

At length the eve of the happy day arrived. The
weather was in all respects propitious, and at daybreak
on the eleventh we set forth, myself and the best and
dearest of all earthly friends long since departed from
this world of toil and trouble, in a light stanhope drawn

by an active horse, encumbered by no luggage beyond our gun-cases and the changes of raiment necessary for our trip.

Old Harry Lee, the sturdy veteran game-keeper, who taught " my young idea how to shoot," and to accompany whom on his rounds I have risen a hundred times from my bed at daybreak or earlier, when the sun rises at three in the morning, had set out two days previously, leading a stout Shetland poney laden with panniers, and taking with him four brace of as staunch and swift and beautiful dogs as ever dropped to shot, or stood staunch and still as death over a running bevy. There were Cynthia and Phebe, a pair of orange and white silky Irish setters, with large soft eyes and coal-black muzzles, feathered six inches deep on the legs and stern—Pierrot and Jason, two liver and white pointers, the former so lively a game-finder that the best shot with whom I ever pulled a trigger was used to say that he " half believed Pierrot could make his own game whenever he was at a loss"—Charon and Pluto, a brace of black and white Russians, fleeced like Arctic bears, and with such a fell of matted wool hang ing over their short bullet heads and grim faces, and almost quenching the light of their quick keen fiery eyes, that it was difficult to conceive how they could see daylight. They were the best retrievers I have ever yet shot over; the staunchest, keenest, most indefatigable and indestructible of dogs.

Charon was for years my own especial dog; him I was allowed to take out of the kennel alone without a keeper to accompany me, when I was, or was supposed to be, too young, too ignorant, and too impetuous to be trusted with any dog that could be damaged. " *Even* Frank," it used to be said, " could not spoil Charon!" and I believe the D—l himself could not, had he tried it.

He had been imperfectly broke, and if birds were killed,

he would run in and fetch them; but even in his unsteadiness he was so staunch, and so unerring was his saga-
city and instinct, that if a fresh bird lay in his route as he
dashed in to fetch that which had fallen, he would invariably point it *dead*. I never knew him flush a single bird
in his most impetuous rushes.

If a covey was missed clean, he would drop sulkily to
charge; but he would invariably look round and stare in your
face with a sort of sullen grunt, as who should say, "What
do you mean by such work as that?" If you missed
three times in succession, menace and coaxing were alike
unavailing. Home went Charon, and for that day was no
more seen.

More extraordinary yet, he could distinguish by the eye
when a hare was wounded, when no man living would
have suspected that the animal was hit; and whereas if
one went away cleanly missed he would charge like a rock,
the instant he perceived, how I cannot imagine, that it
was carrying away a load, he would chase like a devil.
But, as in the other instance, I never saw him chase a hare
that he did not bring it home; and he could no more have
run down a fresh one with a twenty yards start, than I
could run down an elk on an open prairie.

The fourth brace were a pair of coal-black setters,
Death and Dream, beautiful as night which they most re-
sembled, without one white speck on their lustrous coats,
perfectly broken, tractable as lambs, fleet as deer, yet full
of fire and spirit, fearless and tireless, and less fleet only
than the wind.

Such was the governor's kennel; and even as I never yet
have seen such a shot or sportsman as he was, so never have
I seen nor shall I see, so far as I expect, such a kennel of
dogs, whether for staunchness, certainty, speed, or beauty.

All day long we travelled through scenes of the rarest
beauty, by the castled crags of Knaresborough, frowning

over the bright dark waters of the Nid, up the lovely vale of which lay our course to the moorlands—by the old fortalice of Ripley, where the lady Ingolby of that day received Cromwell, when he visited her at the head of his ironsides, with pistols stuck in her apron string—by Hamps thwaite's rural homes, by Dacre pasture and the oak woods of Darley, across Pately bridge and up the brawling Nid unto the spot where Ram's ghyll pours his tributary torrent into the wider stream.

Here, after a homely supper, rashers of bacon, new-laid eggs, short bread and home-brewed ale, to which fatigue had earned us eager appetites, we turned into the coarse clean sheets redolent of the bloomy heather on which they had been bleached, and lulled by the ceaseless brawling of the mountain brook which foamed down its gorge close beneath the window, I, for one, sank asleep so soon as my head touched the pillow, and dreamed of moorcocks until a light flashed before my eyes, a hand was laid heavily upon my shoulder, and the old game-keeper's voice aroused me from my soft slumber.

It was past three o'clock, and breakfast was ready in the parlor. The sun would be up before we could reach the moor, and the morning promised to be a fine one. I was on my feet in an instant, and my first day on the Yorkshire moors had begun—he who will, shall hereafter learn how it ended.

THE YORKSHIRE MOORS—CONCLUDED.

At length the long-wished-for moment had arrived. The breakfast was duly honored, the panniers packed with luncheon, to return as we hoped, packed with moor-fowl, and slung on the Shetland pony, were despatched, together with two brace of dogs, the bitches Cynthia and Phebe, for the morning's work, and the Russians for the afternoon, under the care of the guide, to meet us on the verge of the moors.

It was not yet light when we started from the door of the little Inn, to scale the four miles of steep and continuous ascent, which led by a road liker far to the gulley of a mountain torrent, than to any path made by the hands of man, from the level of the beautiful bright river to the summit of the misty plateau which forms the base of the moors, the loftier hills rising above it in huge, rounded or square-topped masses, divided from each other, sometimes by wide plains of the richest heather, sometimes by mossy bogs, whence steal the rills which, gradually swelling into burns, as the larger brooks are termed, pour down through the ghylls or gorges which they cut for themselves through the peat, the gravel, nay! even through the solid sandstone, and become the feeding tributaries of the lovely rivers of the West Riding

The first pale streaks of dawn stole up the east as we ascended, the clouds, few, fleecy, and far between, hung lightly here and there in the pure dark sky, from which all the stars had faded except Venus, who still showed her waning lamp near the horizon, for she was now the morning star.   As we reached the summit, where two dark, indistinct shapes were awaiting us, of boy and pony, at the swing gate which gave access through the high dry stone wall, to the wild, bare moor, on which many of the smaller landholders of the ghylls and dales had right of pasturage for their black-faced sheep—*in futuro* the finest of mountain mutton—and black cattle in proportion to the number of acres in their respective holdings, though the lord or lady paramount of the manor only has the right of shooting, or deputizing persons to shoot over the range; the gray clouds changed their tints to amber, to rosy-red, to crimson to flaming liquid gold, as the east gradually flushed brighter and brighter, until at length the great sun rushed up

like an orb of burnished gold, through the thin mist on
the mountain heads, and, in an instant it was perfect
day.

What a scene, what a panorama was there;—beneath and
behind us the long retiring valley of the Nid, winding
away in a far perspective of hanging woods, rich emerald
pastures, crofts bordered with their shadowy sycamores,
and village roofs and humble chapels peeping out between,
until lost in the blue mists of distance.

Before us unnumbered leagues of barrenness and desolation, blue mountain beyond blue mountain, rolling away
the vast earth billows of that moorland sea, without a spot
of culture, an oasis of fertility, to the borders of Scotland,
fifty leagues distance to the north-westward.

Around us knolls, hillocks, hummocks, hills, some round,
some sugarloaf, some rock-ribbed and crag-crested; deep
treacherous morasses tempting the foot of the unwary
visitor by their exquisite smoothness, and the unrivalled
richness of their emerald verdure; deep, abrupt, broken
gorges and ravines, with clear brooks brawling along their
bottoms, but all pathless, seemingly untrodden of man,
cursed, one would say, with irredeemable barrenness, and
inhabited only by the few titlarks which faintly hailed the
rising sun with hymns, scarcely audible amid those vast
solitudes, and the snipes and curlews which rose now and
then, screaming dissonantly, from the bogs and peat-holes,
whence the turf had been cut for fuel, for we had not as
yet reached the choicer portion of the moor, haunted alike
by the blackfaced quadrupeds, and the red-grouse allured
ever to the same vicinity by the same succulent food on
which their excellence depends—the young sprouts of the
tenderest short heather, springing fresh from places
over which the fire has run in the latest autumn of the
past year. Nevertheless, with all the desolation, there
was a sort of peculiar wild beauty, arising for the most

part from the singular and variegated hues of the surface;
where the young heather was in bloom the whole super-
fices of hundreds and hundreds of acres was glowing with
the most gorgeous hues of amythyst, garnet, and rubies;
where the dry stalks and sere leaves of the later and older
growth prevailed, all was deep tawney russet; where the
fire had recently passed all was black as charred stumps and
the very peat soil, scorched to the bottom, could make it—
then again, there were patches of green furze with their
golden blossoms, and tracts of dark green, rushy, rank
grass, and gleams of the brightest emerald around the well-
heads, and over all the treacherous morasses.

But now we had reached our opening ground, the boy
with the pony and the second brace of dogs was ordered
to the rear, with instructions to meet us by the side of a
certain gray rock, and spring-head, on the northern edge
of Kettletang, a huge, bluff-headed hill, overtopping all
his neighbors, at noon, when we should be there to refresh
the inner man, and take up the fresh dogs for the afternoon.

This arranged, to work we went. The ground was a long
swell of gentle hillocks, facing the morning and sun, and
sloping gently down to the south-eastward.   It was covered with short purple heather, in full bloom, with here and
there a patch of soft, green grass, and now and then a
well-head, with a small silvery runnel oozing from it, and
showing by the greener and lighter hues of the ling and
grass around its course, how vivifying and beneficial were
its influences.

It was precisely one of those ranges which the young
broods love in the early morning, at the beginning of the
season, and, in fact, the fleet bitches had not ranged five
hundred yards, which they did at full speed, heads up and
sterns down, crossing each other at every five hundred
yards distance, turning unbidden, and quartering their

ground beautifully, before Cynthia came on her game so
suddenly that she literally threw a somersault as she *set*
the birds, turning herself completely over, so that her stern
was toward the brood, and that she pointed them over her
shoulder. Phebe backed her at a quarter of a mile, as
steadily as if she had been cast in bronze or carved in
marble.

"Steady now, Frank !" said the Governor—" They are
close under her nose."

Gingerly, but firmly we advanced, finger-nail on the trig-
ger-guard, thumb on the hammer, till we were within six
paces of the bitch ; she was trembling with intense anxiety,
her eyes gleaming like coals of fire, her brows corrugated,
the slaver on her lip.

"Careful, Frank, careful !" said the Governor, " I fancy
it will prove a brood of squeakers, too young to kill—
don't shoot the old hen, if it be so."

But at the instant, as he spoke, being to the right hand
of me, the old cock rose clapping his wings in defiance,
and uttering a loud crow crossed me to the leftward. He
was a splendid fellow. He rose so close that the bare
scarlet granulated spots about his eyes, and his angrily
erected crest were clearly visible, as well as the golden
and deep red hackles on his neck, and the beautifully pied
plumage of his brown, red, and black-barred back and wing
coverts, his breast was partly turned toward me, and it
was black as night. He proved afterward to be a three
year old bird, and weighed but a few ounces short of four
pounds weight,—for I was steady, let him get fifteen yards
away, then raised my gun deliberately, drew trigger as
the butt touched my shoulder—a stream of feathers drifted
down wind, and with a heavy thud the noble cock fell
dead among the short flowery heather.

Nothing rose at the report, and it was not till after
much kicking and beating of the heather, that the old hen

rose with seventeen squeakers, not bigger than six-weeks chickens.

Them, of course, we bade go their way rejoicing, as we did likewise, specially I—for had I not been cool, even by the Governor's *ipse dixit*, and killed my first heath-cock fairly ?

Our next find was three old bachelors, as they are termed by the initiated, old cock birds, namely, which, not having paired or bred the last year, band together and become great pests to the breeders, beating off the young males, and disturbing the amorous couples.

They rose wild, at long-range—but we sent two snap shots after them, and two fell,—the Governor's killed dead, mine wingtipped, but the bitches retrieved him cleverly after a mile's roading. The third rise was a well grown brood of twelve, with their parents, which also got up shy and distant, the heather being as yet too wet with dew to allow their lying hard. Yet I knocked one over, my father killing two—the old cock, a prodigiously long shot, with his second barrel.

But as the day improved, and the sun grew warmer, the birds lay better, and I did my work creditably, to my own satisfaction, and won moderate praise from the Governor, and huge *kudos* from my preceptor in the noble art of *collineation*, as poor Cypress, Jr., was wont to call it, old Harry Lee.

When we counted heads at luncheon I was only two brace and a half behind my companion, who, as I said, was the best shot, walker and sportsman, it ever was my lot to meet, having bagged my thirteen brace and a half, six brace of them clever double shots, to his sixteen brace.

In the afternoon, with the fresh dogs, though I shot as well, or, considering the change in the weather and state of the game, perhaps better than before luncheon, I did not fare so well.

The day had become overcast, the wind had got up, the grouse had packed, and rose very wild and flew like hawks —still, when the sun set, and we knocked off work, I had shot eleven brace more, three golden plover, and a curlew —but the Governor, who always shot the best when the shooting was the hardest, had bagged seventeen brace more of grouse, a hare, and a brace of mallards, which sprung unexpectedly from a peat bog.

On the whole I had scored twenty-four and a half brace of moor-game, fifty-three head of game in all, against his thirty-three brace of grouse, and total of sixty-nine head —pretty well that for a green hand in his first season, shooting beside one of the best guns in the three kingdoms.

There were twenty-nine guns on the moor that morning, and the Governor beat the two best, with fourteen brace to spare.

Was not I a proud and a happy man that night, when after quaffing a half gallon of new milk, with a modicum of Jamaica in it—was too tired to eat supper—I plunged into the thyme-scented sheets, and was asleep before my head was well on the pillow.

CHAPTER XII.

TREATMENT OF THE DISTEMPER

SINCE the foregoing pages of this little work were prepared, a friend has put us in possession of the following accurate description of the great enemy of the canine race—*the Distemper*. It was written years ago, by the great JENNER, and is, of course, an admirable description of the disease.

Every man has his own cure for the Distemper; the country is full of "infallible recipes." The chief point is to know whether or not the animal really has the disease. If that is *early* discovered, a mild purgative every other day, light diet, and a clean, comfortable kennel will probably cure him.

The following is the *Jenner* article :

DISTEMPER IN DOGS.

That disease among dogs which has familiarly been called "the Distemper," has not hitherto, I believe, been much noticed by medical men. My situation in the country favoring my wishes to make some observations on this singular malady, I availed myself of it during several successive years, among a large number of fox hounds belonging to the Earl of Berkeley ; and from observing how frequently it has been confounded with hydrophobia, I am induced to lay the result of my inquiries before the Medical and Chirurgical Society. It may be difficult, perhaps, precisely to ascertain the period of its first appearance in Britain. In this and the neighboring counties, I have not been able to trace it back much beyond the middle of the last century; but it has since spread universally. I knew a gentleman who, about forty-five years ago, destroyed the greater part of his hounds, from supposing them mad, when the distemper first broke out among them; so little was it then known by those most conversant with dogs. On the continent, I find it has been known for a much longer period. It is as contagious among dogs as the small-pox, measles, or scarlet fever among the human species; and the contagious miasmata, like those arising from the diseases just mentioned, retain their infectious properties a long time after separation from the distempered animal. Young hounds, for example, brought in a state of health into a kennel where others have gone through the distemper, seldom escape it. I have endeavored to destroy the contagion, by ordering every part of the kennel to be carefully washed with water, then white washed, and finally to be repeatedly fumigated with the vapor of marine acid; but without any good result.

The dogs generally sicken early in the second week after exposure to the contagion. It is more commonly a violent disease than otherwise, and cuts off, at least, one in the three that are attacked by it. It commences with inflammation of the substance of the lungs, and generally of the mucous membrane of the bronchiæ. The inflammation at the same time seizes on the membranes of the nostrils, and those lining the bones of the nose; particularly the nasal portion of the ethmoid bone. These membranes are often inflamed to such a degree, as to cause extravasation of blood, which I have observed coagulated on their surface. The breathing is short and quick, and the breath is often fetid. The teeth are covered with dark-looking mucus. There is frequently a vomiting of a

glary fluid. The dog commonly refuses food, but his
thirst seems insatiable, and nothing seems to cheer him
like the sight of water. The bowels, though generally
constipated as the disease advances, are frequently affected
with the diarrhœa at its commencement. The eyes are
inflamed; and the sight is often obscured by mucus secreted from the eye-lids, or by opacity of the cornea. The
brain is often affected as early as the second day after the
attack. The animal becomes stupid, and his general
habits are changed. In this state, if not prevented by
loss of strength, he sometimes wanders from his home.
He is frequently endeavoring to expel, by forcible expir-
ations, the mucus from the trachea and fauces, with a
peculiar rattling noise. His jaws are generally smeared
with it, and it sometimes flows out in a frothy state, from
his frequent champing. During the progress of the disease, especially in its advanced stages, he is disposed to
bite and gnaw anything within his reach. He has sometimes epileptic fits, or quick succession of general, though
slight convulsive spasms of the muscles.

If the dog survives, this affection of the muscles con
tinues through life. He is often attacked with fits of a
different description. He first staggers, then tumbles,
rolls, cries as if whipped, and tears up the ground with
his teeth and fore feet. He then lies down senseless and
exhausted. On recovering he gets up, moves his tail,
looks placid, comes to a whistle, and appears in every
respect much better than before the attack. The eyes,
during this paroxysm, look bright, and unless previously
rendered dim by mucus, or opacity of the cornea, seem as
if they were starting from the sockets. He becomes ema-
ciated, and totters from feebleness in attempting to walk,
or from a partial paralysis of the hind legs. In this state,
he sometimes lingers on until the third or fourth week, and
then either begins to show signs of returning health (which

seldom happens when the symptoms have continued with this degree of violence) or expires. During convalescence, he has sometimes, though rarely, profuse hæmorrhage from the nose. When the inflammation of the lungs is very severe, he frequently dies on the third day. I knew one instance of a dog's dying within twenty-four hours after the seizure, and in that short space of time the greater portion of the lungs was, from exudation, converted into a substance nearly as solid as the liver of a sound animal. In this case, the liver itself was considerably inflamed, and the eyes and flesh universally were tinged with yellow, though I did not observe anything obstructing the biliary ducts. In other instances, I have also observed the eyes looking yellow.

The above is a description of the disease in its severest form; but in this, as in the diseases of the human body, there is every gradation in its violence. There is also another affinity to some human diseases, viz., that the animal which has once gone through it, very rarely meets with a second attack. Fortunately, this distemper is not communicable to man. Neither the effluvia from the diseased dog, nor the bite, has proved in any instance infectious; but as it has often been confounded with canine madness, as I have before observed, it is to be wished that it were more generally understood; for those who are bitten by a dog in this state, are sometimes thrown into such perturbation, that hydrophobic symptoms have actually arisen from the workings of the imagination. Mr. John Hunter used to speak of a case somewhat of this description in his lectures.* Having never, to a certainty,

* A gentleman who received a severe bite from a dog, soon after fancied the animal was mad. He felt a horror at the sight of liquids, and was actually convulsed on attempting to swallow them. So uncontrollable were his prepossessions, that Mr. Hunter conceived that he would have died, had not the dog which inflicted the wound been

seen a dog with hydrophobia, I am of course unable to lay down a positive criterion for distinguishing between that disease and the distemper, in the precise way I could wish; but if the facts have been correctly stated, that in hydrophobia the eye of the dog has more than ordinary vivacity in it, and, as the term implies, he refuses to take water, and shudders even at the sight of it, while in the distemper he looks dull and stupid, is always seeking after water, and never satisfied with what he drinks, there can be no loss for a ready discriminating line between the two diseases.

March 21, 1809.

fortunately found and brought into his room in perfect health. This soon restored his mind to a state of tranquillity. The sight of water no longer affected him, and he quickly recovered.

CHAPTER XIII.

SNIPE SHOOTING IN FLORIDA.

BY COR DE CHASSE.

As this little volume was getting ready for the press, the following interesting and graphic paper, on *Snipe Shooting in Florida,* reached me from that accomplished gentleman and crack shot, Col. WM. T. STOCKTON, known to the readers of the *N. Y. Spirit of the Times* as " COR DE CHASSE :"

" QUINCY, Fla., January 26th, 1856.

"MY DEAR HOOPER :—I am only at home a few days, and I am sure you will forgive me for my seeming neglect, when I tell you that I was absent from home for nearly three months, and had so much to say to wife and bairns on my return. But somewhat to my surprise, I *did* find your note requiring 'that article.' Since I have announced that it was from the veritable 'Jones,' I have become a man of more note. True, I was Intendant of the town, and Captain of the Quincy Light Horse, but the splendor of even those brilliant titles paled before the new one, of a correspondent of 'the author of Simon Suggs,' and 'Editor of Montgomery Mail.' But, really, your request is so flattering, you have the gift, as Pliny has it, (I'll quote him again shortly) '*adornare verbis, benefacta,*' that though little in the mood (though I have been much in the *mud* of late), I must make the effort—

I labor under the difficulty of not knowing what sort of
an article you want, or to what use you wish to put it.
If it don't suit, why fires are never far off this cold
weather."

                *   *   *   *   *   *   *   *

" But I promised to tell you something of our Snipe
shooting here in Florida, and if other kinds of sport become mingled with it, it is because, from the very nature
of the shooting ground it follows as a consequence. I do
not propose to give you a scientific dissertation on the bird
in question, for Audubon, Wilson, Frank Forester, &c.,
have given us all that can be wished. I will simply
sketch the proceedings of a friend and myself, during a
couple of days in the beginning of December before last.
P. and Cor have hunted the deer and worked their pointers together for some fifteen years. ' Cor,' said P., ' let
us have our trip to Lake Jackson, and see if ducks and
snipe are as numerous as heretofore ; the cold weather, I
am sure, has brought in the ducks, and in this bright sun-
shine the snipe will lie like quail.'

" ' Agreed, we'll start to-morrow at dawn ; the ponies
will make a capital team on the road ; we'll take saddles
with us, and use them in going from camp to the shooting-
ground and back. Sam will do the needful for the horses
and the camp, for he has been with us so often, he has all
the wrinkles from a venison steak up to a roasted snipe.'

" The next morning as the grey showed itself in the
East, we were on the road. The hunting wagon was
well arranged. The mess-chest supplied with all we
could require (I am afraid to go into particulars since
the 'Major' came out in 'the Spirit' with his tirade against
demijohns), forming the seat of the driver Sam, who
handled the gallant ponies, matched in action, though
awfully diverse in color, as if to the 'manner born ' while

Don and Donis ' charged' under our seat in the after part of the wagon."

" ' Shall we reconsider the motion to ' camp' and go to the Governor's ?' asked Cor. ' Oh ! let's camp by all means ; as we shall be so much in the mud and water, there will be less of restraint on us. True, the Governor will not forgive us, but my voice is for a camp at Shepard's old Sugar Mill ; there we will find a roof to cover us, and it will be hard if the old timbers don't furnish us fuel.' "

" Two hours of time, and the quick moving ponies, placed us across Little River and the Ocklockonee, and the waters of Lake Jackson were before us. And, now, let me sketch this paradise of the snipe-shooter. It was originally some twelve miles in length, by from one to two in breadth, and its bright waters shone clear in the sunlight, from highland to highland, but in the *progress* of the age, whether from new subterranean outlets effected, which discharge the waters more rapidly, or from the greater evaporation, arising from the clearing up of its shores, certain it is, that with the exception of a few eccentric changes, its level has been lowering, and in localities where formerly we had capital trout-fishing in six feet water, at present large crops of the Indian corn are produced, subject of course to the accident of an occasional overflow, in which case, if the corn is ripened, instead of the wagon drawn by patient oxen, boats worked by ' darkies' in a hurry, become the medium of transportation of the crop to the crib. It is on these flats we seek the snipe ; if a rise has taken place in the Lake, followed by a withdrawal of the waters, the tufts of grass among the corn form capital cover for the ' Scolopaces,' but in many places, when the land has not been brought into cultivation, a kind of marsh grass springs up, in which the game will lie to a dog as well as sportsmen can wish. But you must bear in mind that these same shooting-

grounds afford full feed to the Brent, Black duck, Mallard,
Grey duck, Teal, *et id omne genus.* The highlands around
the lake are crowned with handsome residences, and the
youthful sportsman may almost hope that his skill is
looked upon and admired by ladies fair, even should they
fail to recognise him on account of the sepia tinge he may
have acquired from a plunge into an alligator bed, or some
similar " causa teterrima *belli*," anglice, going *almost* waist
deep into a mud hole.

" The deserted sugar-house has been reached, the ponies
rubbed down, and after a light feed, saddled for our use ;
full directions for the arrangements of the camp given,
and Don and Donis, with wistful faces, are begging us to
be off. Hardly had we gone fifty paces when several
snipe rose wild, with the old familiar ' scape, scape.' Two
of them doubled back, high in air, and though going
down wind like bullets, were handsomely nailed by Cor
and his friend, much to the astonishment of a passing
countryman, whose wonder found vent in the words ' I
tell *you !*' as the birds were carefully retrieved by the
well trained dogs. ' Let's try the point next the Governor's.' We found it in just the right order. The grass
was some six inches high, affording an excellent cover for
our game, while the rich black loam, though affording sufficiently good footing for the sportsman, was all that the
most difficult snipe could desire in the way of feeding-
ground. You may imagine the prospect of our sport
when I tell you, that on this point there were about fifty
acres, almost identical in character, and we knew of sundry
other similar places. Pity 'tis that we cannot dwell (as in
deer-hunting, on the music of the pack, the turns and shifts
of the game, as hill and valley echo with the cry) on the
gallant action of the pointers—there is no time. They
found almost at the same moment. ' You see to Donis,
I'll go to Don.' Before I could reach my dog I saw

feathers floating on the wind, while the reports of P's barrels reached my ear, 'Scape,' and a snipe rose almost from under my feet, and was fairly missed from the unsportsmanlike flurry in which I fired. Still the good dog held his point. The load was quickly replaced. This time there was no hurry, and as three or four snipe rose within ten feet of Don's nose, two were easily cut down. For an hour the sport was fine—never did snipe lie so close; hardly could we walk them up—occasionally, the warning cry 'mark duck,' 'mark brent,' 'up lake' or 'down' would be given, and shooters and dogs crouch low, and reasonably close shots be obtained. In spite of number seven shot (light missles for heavy game) at intervals, a brent would come wizzing through the air with a broken wing, or a mallard strike the soft ground with a 'thud' right grateful to the ear. (Do not be critical on our number seven shot; we find them small enough for snipe, and they *will* kill a duck). But all this was the poetry of our work. Soon the snipe found the open too uncomfortable and took refuge in bushy thickets which skirted a portion of the lake, the shrubs rising to a height of from six to ten feet. Here there was no grass, and nothing but the excellence of our dogs enabled us to accomplish anything. The birds rose wild, and snap-shots were all the fashion, and at least one-half the time the dogs knew better than the men whether the bird was killed or missed. But without even the effort at a boast, well did the 'Mullin' in the hands of Cor, and the English gun in those of his friend, do their duty—of course, at intervals the sportsmen would meet and a few minutes halt be made to rest and compare notes. 'Do you see, across the lake, that little cove,' said Cor, 'where that fine live oak and the low pines shade the very bank? There, last winter, that party of our young friends made their first camp on the lake. As an old hand, I received a pressing invitation to

join them at some period of the week of their sojourn.
On the morning after they reached camp, business called
me within a few miles of them, I thought I would drop in
and see what they had done. The party had just come in
to lunch, and as they caught sight of me a shout was raised,
and they advanced to meet me. Among them was 'the
General.' "What sport?" "Pretty fair!" but I could
remark an appearance of elation in them all, though most
marked, perhaps, in " the General," and so quietly waited
for the *dénouement.* A surprise for me was evidently preparing. The General's military step assumed a prouder
air, as he strode beside my horse; a scientific wheel was
accomplished around the tent, by which the game was
suddenly made visible. "What do you think of that?"
triumphantly asked the General. " By Jupiter, P," continued Cor, if they didn't have twenty-three Blue Peters
laid out side by side, and not one single other bird !
Commanding my countenance, I inquired " how it had
been done?" " Oh ! all military science ! it *will* tell ! I
discovered the flock in the cove there, at daylight, arranged
the hunters at once, an ambuscade was formed surrounding the cove, and at the signal, the whole battalion, I
should say, partly fired; only three escaped ! as we shall be
here several days yet, and it will not do to risk their spoil-
ing, what had we best do with them?' I could see that
a misgiving was creeping over the whole of them which
was fully confirmed by my reply, 'Hide them, as soon as
possible, lest some sportsman should pass this way.' There
were no more Blue Peters killed on that hunt—(The blue
Peter, with its half-webbed feet, its chicken-like bill, its
strong odor, and its absolute tameness, is always spared
by the duck-shooter). 'But,' Cor went on, how splend-
idly our dogs have behaved. I always knew that Don
was the best dog I ever hunted over, but I now believe
Donis is the best I ever saw,' 'Donis understands you

evidently,' returned P., ' and is expressing his thanks, by that wag of his tail; we have sent the remnant of the snipe, for the most part, back to the open ground, let us have another turn at them and then we must change our shot for the evening flight of the ducks,' and well did man and dog and gun do their work. The sport was so good, the birds lay so well, the ground so open, that shooting fully in sight of each other, we did not *dare* to miss. There was no need to profit by the peculiarities of the game, as derived from Frank Forester's valued information. The shooting was better up wind than down, as it gave the dogs a better chance. Sunday visits had been paid to the game-bags, on the ponies, but our pockets were again becoming onerous. It was now sundown and we hurried to them once more, emptied pockets, and changed shot, Cor adopting No. 4, while P. preferred No. 6, and supported his judgment by saying ' we'll catch the mallard coming in to feed, and there will be few long shots.' We took stands on opposite sides of an arm of the Lak, about seventy-five yards wide, which expanded into a bay, filled with water-grasses, lily-pads, &c.—a portion of a field of corn had been submerged, also, offering great temptation to the green heads and their mates. By the time, we were safely ensconced in the tall grass, with the dogs couching near us, P. sang out 'mark ducks—lakewards!' and from that time forward, we had enough to keep us busy.

"Night closed in, but still the flashes of our guns at intervals lighted up the grassy waters, while the responsive 'plash' told that, even in that uncertain light, we were doing execution. ' Up rose the yellow moon,' and by her beams the shooting still went on. Of course, there were no long shots even attempted; but so unsuspiciously did the mallard come in, that the firing was well-sustained. In the long, coarse rushes, the saw-grass, the lily-pads, and the cold water, our thin-skinned pointers of course failed to

retrieve many of the birds; but when, after nearly two
hours of the moonlight shooting, we gave it up, tired and
chilled, the dogs shivering, and the guns foul, we each had
as many as we could well carry to our horses. Securing
our game to the saddles, we hurried to camp. Sam had
managed admirably; a brilliant fire threw its broad glare
over the ruins; by propping a shed, a safe shelter was
provided for our horses; a quantity of fennel had been
gathered, and with the blankets spread over it, an easy
and fragrant bed was ready for us. But now 'spirits
were called from the vasty deep'—(aye, and they came,
too)—of the demijohn, much needed, believe me, after that
night's exposure in the marsh, with the ice forming in the
still pools. Wet clothes and boots were exchanged for
dry, and things were more comfortable—*nunc edendum*.
In the excitement of the sport, we had forgotten that
breakfast had been had before day, and that nothing had
been eaten in the interval. The ham and chicken were
duly paraded, but Cor was bound to have some of the
'scapers' cooked *en papillote*, sundry stationery having
been provided with a view to this important matter. Half
a dozen snipe were duly plucked by Sam, while the ex-
change of wet clothes for dry was being made; and with
all due deference to Frank Forester, a modicum of butter,
salt, and pepper *was* placed within each before they were
encased in the virgin-white costume, which duly encircled
them before they were consigned to—ashes. The ten
minutes were carefully noted, the plates judiciously heated,
the toast anxiously waited, while the operation proceeded
under the skilful ministry of Sam (a ministry about to
become general, I trust.) Those ten minutes gave us
time to count our game, for the spirit of rivalry still main-
tained. 'How many snipe, Cor?' 'Wait till I get
through——sixty-eight.' 'You have beaten me; I have
only fifty-six—but I expected it would be so. How about

ducks?' Cor counted out twenty-three ducks and three brent. It was now P.'s turn. 'Hold on! twenty-six, twenty-seven, twenty-eight, twenty-nine, and all told, and two brent.' 'That makes a grand total for the day, after the twenty miles' ride, of one hundred and twenty-four snipe, fifty-two ducks, and five brent! What a glorious show they make! We drink to Lake Jackson and the glorious sport we have had!' 'Snipe ready, sar,' reported Sam, as he placed the long-bills on the impromptu table. 'Delmonico' was nowhere; not an odor or aroma lost! Ye gods! did *you* ever eat snipe, cooked in camp *en papillote?* Never, I am sure, or ambrosia would not have been heard of! As we puffed the *post-cœnal* cigar, our conversation naturally turned on our game and its habits. 'You were not with the Doctor and myself last spring,' remarked Cor, 'when the snipe acted so singularly, on that piece of wet land in the Stephens' branch. I presume few sportsmen can say what we can. There are but very few I would even ask to believe me. We shot the English snipe, the veritable *scolopax wilsonii*, while sitting in tops of trees, an hundred feet in air! Think of that, Master Brooks. While out quail-shooting, we found about a dozen snipe in this place. They were wild as deer; nor dog nor sportsman could approach them. After flushing them once or twice, without getting a shot, away they all went, as if about to emigrate finally. Higher and higher they whirled in air, till the eye could scarcely follow them. This continued for some six or eight minutes, when back they came, apparently in as much of a hurry as when they left. Three or four came to the ground as usual; but imagine our surprise when we saw the rest lighting in the tops of tall trees. We waived all sporting rules, to be able to say that we had killed snipe thus.' The cigars were finished. 'One smile,' said P., 'for a night-cap, and then to bed: we must be out by day-break, to pick up the

ducks we lost to-night, or the hawks will be before us.
So we turned in, but not for long. P. had forgotten that
two or three strong smiles, indulged in with an empty
stomach, might result in something serious. A peculiar
sound disturbed the quiet of the camp. It was evidently
a throe (throw ?) of nature. 'What's the matter ?' 'Sick,'
gasped P. 'What can be the cause ?' 'Those d——d
snipe !' Cor subsided among the blankets. All that sympathy *could* do was to control the risibles. And for a
while he listened to the quack-qua-ack, quack, quack, of
the mallard on the lake, and the cry of the brent as they
passed overhead. Even the 'scape' of the snipe came
sharply through the deep stillness of night. These sounds
mingling with his dreams, made his night a restless one,
for the triggers *would* creep, and the *hammers* would *not*
fall. 'Turn out Cor,' (he was whistling the reveille) 'I
have recovered from those *snipe*, and we must go and see
about the ducks our dogs failed to retrieve. Let's have a
cup of coffee and be off.' The dogs were fed with some
warm corn-bread, to comfort them in the cold work to be
done ; and it *was* cold work, breaking the scale of ice on
the grassy bay, as the sportsmen found it, for they had to
take water freely to encourage the dogs.

"Right gallantly did the pointers perform service only
fit for the rough-haired Newfoundland. Seventeen more
ducks were recovered by them, though in some cases the
hawks disputed the property, quite sharply. Back to
camp, to breakfast, and the snipe served as before, were
followed by no such dire results, as on the previous night.
'We have all the game we want,' suggested P. for ourselves and friends, to continue is murder; let's go home.'
'The sun has come out bright and warm,' interposed
Cor, 'I think the trout will rise—I have with me, the
Whitehall spinning squid, and if you will paddle me, I'll
ensure a Catholic Friday dinner in Quincy.' 'All right,

there's a skiff at the landing, which, with a little bailing,
will suit our purpose." "I done found a fishing pole" put
in, Sam. Instead of using an hundred yards of line, as the
inventor of the artificial bait contemplated, rod, we, owing
to the grassy water of the lake, limited our aspirations to
eighteen inches of a stout cord, which secured to the end
of the rod, enabled us to play the glancing bait, in front
of the boat—at first, the fates were unpropitious, but as
the sun grew warmer, a change came over the waters—a
rush, a flash, and a three pound trout lay in the bottom of
the skiff, and now the sport became most exciting. Sometimes the rush was made from the depths below, and all
the previous notice given was the dash so vigorously made,
that the pearly drops fell in board; at others, as some
cunning old fellow, hidden near the surface, under a lily-
pad, and anxious for his breakfast, dashed to secure the
illusive bait (he found it, not "vox" but "hooks et
praeterea nihil,") the water would swell for a length of
perhaps twenty feet. Talk of your Salmon-fishing at the
rate of one a day! one hour of that incessant rush, dash,
flash, splash, was worth an age of fly-whipping. The
weights ran from one to eight or ten pounds. (Please in-
duce some icthyologist to tell us the true name of this fish.
I will furnish drawings and *count the fins* and *fin-spines*,
for any one who will enlighten us. Black perch, I call
them, when playing scientific.) "And now for a full count of
the results," said P. "One hundred and twenty-four snipe,
sixty-nine ducks, five brent and twenty-eight trout which
will weigh over one hundred pounds! when this sport is
exceeded, "may we be there to see!" Sam, put to the
ponies—while we smile once more to the paradise of the
snipe shooter, Lake Jackson."

January 26, 1856.   COR DE CHASSE.

GARDENING FOR PROFIT,

In the Market and Family Garden.

By Peter Henderson.

FINELY ILLUSTRATED.

This is the first work on Market Gardening ever published in this country. Its author is well known as a market gardener of eighteen years' successful experience. In this work he has recorded this experience, and given, without reservation, the methods necessary to the profitable culture of the commercial or

MARKET GARDEN.

It is a work for which there has long been a demand, and one which will commend itself, not only to those who grow vegetables for sale, but to the cultivator of the

FAMILY GARDEN,

to whom it presents methods quite different from the old ones generally practiced. It is an ORIGINAL AND PURELY AMERICAN work, and not made up, as books on gardening too often are, by quotations from foreign authors.

Every thing is made perfectly plain, and the subject treated in all its details, from the selection of the soil to preparing the products for market.

CONTENTS.

Men fitted for the Business of Gardening.
The Amount of Capital Required, and
Working Force per Acre.
Profits of Market Gardening.
Location, Situation, and Laying Out.
Soils, Drainage, and Preparation.
Manures, Implements.
Uses and Management of Cold Frames.
Formation and Management of Hot-beds.
Forcing Pits or Green-houses.
Seeds and Seed Raising.
How, When, and Where to Sow Seeds.
Transplanting, Insects.
Packing of Vegetables for Shipping.
Preservation of Vegetables in Winter.
Vegetables, their Varieties and Cultivation.

In the last chapter, the most valuable kinds are described, and the culture proper to each is given in detail.

Sent post-paid, price $1.50.

ORANGE JUDD & CO., 41 Park Row, New-York.